Bulletin 394
KIT Development Policy & Practice

Facilitating pro-poor business

Why advice goes further when it's backed by investment

Michiel Arnoldus, John Belt, Marije Boomsma, Maurits de Koning, Anna Laven, Lucian Peppelenbos, Bart de Steenhuijsen Piters, Kees-Jan van Til, and Hugo Verkuijl

Colophon

Bulletins of the Royal Tropical Institute (KIT)
The KIT Bulletin Series deals with current themes in international development. It is a multi-disciplinary forum for scientists, policy makers, managers and development advisors in agriculture, natural resource managements, health, culture, history and anthropology to present their work. These fields reflect the broad scope of KIT's activities.

KIT Development Policy & Practice
KIT Development Policy & Practice is the Royal Tropical Institute's main department for international development. Our aim is to contribute to reducing poverty and inequality in the world and to support sustainable development. We carry out research and provide advisory services and training in order to build and share knowledge on a wide range of development issues. We work in partnership with higher education, knowledge and research institutes, non-governmental and civil society organizations, and responsible private enterprises in countries around the world.

Contact information
Royal Tropical Institute (KIT)
KIT Development Policy & Practice
PO Box 95001
1090 HA Amsterdam
The Netherlands
Telephone: +31 (0)20 568 8458
Fax: +31 (0)20 568 8444
Email: A.Laven@kit.nl
Website: www.kit.nl/development

© 2011 KIT, Amsterdam, The Netherlands

KIT Publishers
Mauritskade 63
Postbus 95001
1090 HA Amsterdam
www.kitpublishers.nl
publishers@kit.nl

This is an open-access publication distributed under the terms of the Creative Commons Attribution License, which permits unrestricted use, distribution, and reproduction in any medium, provided the original author and source are credited.

Edited by Robert Wagner
Cover and design Grafisch ontwerpbureau Agaatsz bNO, Meppel, The Netherlands
Pictures by Michiel Arnoldus, Marije Boomsma, Bart de Steenhuijsen-Piters, Kees-Jan van Til and Hugo Verkuijl
Printing Bariet, Ruinen, The Netherlands

Keywords

Pro-poor business, facilitator, sustainable investment.

ISBN 978 94 6022 155 2

Table of contents

Preface — 5
What is this bulletin about? — 5
Who is the bulletin for? — 6
Parts of the bulletin — 6
How was the book produced? — 6
   The writeshop process — 6
   Writeshop advantages — 7

1 Facilitating pro-poor businesses — 9
Introduction — 9
The role of the facilitator — 9
Changing position, responsibilities and challenges of actors involved in
pro-poor businesses — 11
   Private sector — 11
   Producers and local traders — 14
   Public sector — 15
   NGOs and donors — 16
   Tensions between different actors — 16

2 Bridging business and development – in practice — 19

Case 1. Sourcing ginger from Sierra Leone: no success without transparency and communication. — 21
   Introduction — 21
   Reviving the ginger industry — 21
   Need for a full mandate — 25
   Inclusion of small producers — 25
   Communication and leadership is to be blamed — 26
   The future — 26

Case 2. Supporting sustainable tuna fishing in Ghana — 27
   Introduction — 27
   Starting a new partnership — 27
   Exploratory stage — 28
   KIT's evolving roles — 31
   Pro-poor impact – more potential than facts so far — 32
   Achieving transparency — 33

Case 3. Organic Cocoa Dominican Republic S.A. — 35
   Introduction — 35
   The start-up process — 35
   KIT Reflections on changing roles — 38
   Pro-poor business vs. conventional business approaches — 38

Case 4. Processing biodiesel from jatropha with smallholders in Mali — 41
   Overview — 41
   How a biofuel business was born — 41
   Jatropha goes global — 42
   Overcoming constraints — 44
   KIT's changing role — 45
   Designing for pro-poor impact — 45
   Towards good governance — 33

Case 5. Yiriwa SA: Setting up a trade house for organic products made in Mali — 47
   Introduction — 47
   Growing organic – responding to demand — 47
   KIT reflections — 49
   KIT's changing role: from advisor to active shareholder — 53
   Seeking pro-poor impact — 54
   Governance — 55

3 Facilitating pro-poor businesses: what have we learned? — 57
   Lessons from cases — 57
      Changing positions of pro-poor business partners — 59
      The involvement of a knowledge institute in pro-poor business — 60
   Contextualizing roles — 61
   Final reflections — 63

Epilogue — 65
   Common problems with business plans — 67
   A local network in the South is crucial — 68
   Public funding is needed — 68
   New investments — 69
   The future — 69

Resources — 71

Preface

In development cooperation there is a trend the private sector is seen as an integral part of the solution to reduce poverty. As a result public-private partnerships (PPPs) and pro-poor businesses emerge, involving actors such as private businesses, the public sector, farmer organizations and NGOs. Both modalities are increasingly popular in the field of international development cooperation, corporate social responsibility and sustainable development. PPPs can be defined broadly as an arrangement in which a government and a private entity, for-profit or non-profit, jointly perform or undertake a traditionally public activity (Savas 2005).
A dominant assumption is that in these kinds of partnerships the public sector can learn more from the private sector in terms of efficiency, orientation towards results, and flexibility than the other way around. In contrast, in a pro-poor business the focus is more on mutual learning and interdependency. A pro-poor business is structured as a social enterprise. In this bulletin the focus will be on the latter modality.
A social enterprise can take different forms. It can involve businesses that support social aims ('charity shops') or organizations that support social or environmental aims through their operations (Boomsma 2009). There are some challenges in bringing different actors together in a social enterprise. Each actor (or sector) has its own culture, skills, beliefs and values. In addition, values and goals of the different actors change over time and are not always clear from the start. These differences can cause tensions between the different actors. Generally, there is a need for a facilitator to align interests, bridge cultural differences, fill in gaps in skills, and deal with power differences, wrong expectations and prejudice.

The Royal Tropical Institute (KIT) has experience in playing this role. But over time our role has changed. From being an advisor with little mandate to act and no ownership, to becoming an active shareholder of pro-poor businesses. We have learned that each type of facilitating role has its advantages and disadvantages, and that there are many factors a good facilitator needs to take into account when bringing together the public and private sector and civil society to form a pro-poor business. For KIT this has been a powerful experience, with many ups and downs. This bulletin shares our experiences as a facilitator and pro-poor business engineer with you.

What is this bulletin about?

Systematizing knowledge and practical tools for engaging companies in sustainable poverty alleviation is a key objective of KIT. This book focuses on our own involvement in pro-poor business engineering, and provides a unique opportunity to reflect on our experiences. It also helps us adapt to new circumstances and share insights. By identifying good practices, developing replicable models and tools to guide practice elsewhere, and by disseminating the results to a wider audience, we aim to contribute to successful pro-poor business engineering.

Who is the bulletin for?

This bulletin is especially interesting for development practitioners who fulfil a role as facilitator, but also everyone who aims at bringing the world of development cooperation together with the world of business.

Parts of the bulletin

The remaining chapters in this bulletin focus on partnerships as an instrument for pro-poor business engineering and the role of the facilitator in these partnerships, illustrated by five case-studies.

Chapter 1 Facilitating pro-poor business describes the changing position, responsibilities and challenges of the different actors involved in pro-poor businesses. It also explains the need for a facilitator in pro-poor business engineering and the different roles a facilitator can play.

Chapter 2 Bridging business and development – in practice. This chapter presents five cases of pro-poor business engineering in which KIT plays the role of facilitator, albeit in different forms.

Chapter 3 Facilitating pro-poor businesses: what have we learned? This chapter gives an overview of lessons learned from the different cases. It reflects upon the changing roles played by facilitators in pro-poor business and contextualizes their roles. Finally, we draw some conclusions for the role KIT plays in pro-poor business engineering and the steps forward

Epilogue.

Resources.

How was the book produced?

The writeshop process
The writeshop approach is a participatory method to produce publications first introduced by the International Institute for Rural Reconstruction (IIRR). KIT adapted this approach and together with IIRR published three books: **Chain empowerment** (2006), **Trading up** (2008) and **Value Chain Finance: beyond Microfinance for Rural entrepreneurs** (2010). Our positive experience with this approach has made us decide to use the method for systemizing our own learning process within KIT.

The first step was organizing an internal writeshop with our KIT chain team. The objective was to extract lessons from our involvement in pro-poor business engineering and see how these lessons can be applied and disseminated among a wider audience.

There were a few challenges; first, we were constrained in time, meaning that the process of writing had to be continued after the writeshop. Second, the framework that underlies this book was presented only after a first draft of the cases was already delivered. The introduction of the framework in a later stage has slowed down the process of structuring the cases according to this framework.

In preparation of the writeshop all participants wrote a paper describing a pro-poor business case they had been involved in, using a life-cycle approach.

The first day, the different cases were presented and discussed page by page. The second day, working in a group, the main conclusions from each case and more general lessons for KIT were identified and written down. On this day a framework was proposed, on the basis of which the cases could be analysed. We agreed upon using a facilitator matrix which enabled us to identify the different roles a facilitator can play. This framework is described in Chapter 1.

Writeshop advantages
Although our writeshop was an abbreviated version of earlier writeshops, some of the benefits remain the same. It provided an opportunity to learn about each other's work in the new KIT value chain team, and exchange ideas and experiences. This has contributed to a process of team building. The 'closed' character of the workshop, with only KIT team members, contributed to an informal and open atmosphere making it possible to discuss more sensitive issues and ethical considerations.

1 Facilitating pro-poor businesses

By Michiel Arnoldus and Anna Laven

Introduction

The private sector is the main engine of growth and an important driver of pro-poor growth. Pro-poor private sector development includes and benefits the poor. Often (temporarily) it also involves other actors such as NGOs. For example they play a role in linking poor farmers to profitable markets. The public sector in many cases plays an enabling role by fostering a supportive policy and institutional environment for the business to flourish.

In recent discussions on 'pro-poor businesses' a lot of attention is given to its impact and how to measure it (e.g. Round Table discussions on 'pro-poor' investment funds; different organisations in Boomsma 2009). But, many pro-poor businesses are still in an initial phase and face considerable challenges in the process of establishing themselves. Therefore, in this bulletin the focus is on the process of pro-poor business engineering and the position of the different actors involved in this partnership.

One of the challenges of setting-up a pro-poor business is that all actors involved need to gain something. However, creating mutual benefit can be difficult, and in addition to a common goal, incentives need to be present for all actors involved in the partnership. Also, compromises need to be made for the greater good. In the case of pro-poor businesses all partners must acknowledge the importance of poverty alleviation as well as a commercially viable project, and must be willing to make compromises and contribute resources to reach those goals.

The different interests of the actors involved and the challenges they face, can cause tensions between the different groups. Tennyson and Wilde (2000: p14) mention four key characteristics of a successful and effective partnership, where they put large emphasis on who and what is driving the partnership:

1 Risks and benefits are shared.
2 Principles of openness and equity are upheld; while all those involved may not be equally powerful or resource-rich, each has rights and deserves respect.
3 The partnerships adapt to change.
4 The partnership works towards empowerment.

Someone must take the lead in drawing together the partners and build and cement their working relationship. A facilitator that brokers between the interest of the producers, businesses and non-profit organizations can take up this role.

The role of the facilitator

A facilitator explores where there is common ground, but also understands the different interests, and knows how to align them. When needed, a facilitator offers leadership, but becomes less involved when other partners become too passive and/or loose their sense of ownership.

Ideally, a facilitator recognizes the strengths and limitations of the different actors involved, which helps him/her to define the best role of the partners. Furthermore, a facilitator can structure the governance of the business in a way that safeguards commercial interests and the interests of the poor. This process is what KIT refers to as 'pro poor business engineering'.

A broker or facilitator acts as an intermediary between different parties. A facilitator needs to understand the interests of the parties involved, create mutual understanding between them and negotiate some kind of agreement or "deal". The more complex a partnership, the more vital the facilitator's role is. In particular a facilitator:
- acts as an intermediary and builds collaboration between the partners.
- inspires others in the initiating organizations and partner organizations to follow the partnership approach.
- encourages the adoption of behaviours to help the partnership to function effectively and grow.
- protects the principles and vision of the partnership.

There are different types of facilitators. In this bulletin we make a distinction between being an **Advisor, Mediator, Finance investor** or **Active shareholder**. This categorization is based on differences in 'mandate' versus differences in 'physical ownership'. With 'mandate' we mean that the facilitator has been given authorization to act by all parties involved. 'Physical ownership' is based on equity participation. Equity participation can result in decision-making power, but this is not necessarily the case.

There are four kinds of situations in which facilitators can find themselves, which are depicted in figure 1.1.

Figure 1.1 The facilitator matrix

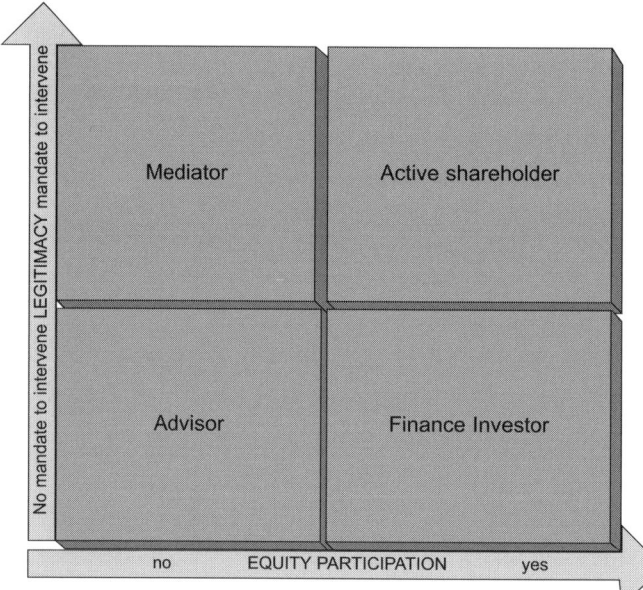

Source: composed by authors

The four different roles are:
1. An **Advisor** is generally an expert to whom the partners look for guidance. An advisor can offer a fresh perspective. Because they do not have direct own interest the advisor can be regarded as neutral, although they will have to proof objectiveness and build trust. As facilitator, an advisor has no decision-making power. Furthermore, an advisor has no mandate to act pro-actively and has to stick to the boundaries set in the assignment.
2. **Mediators** differ from the advisor because they have the mandate to initiate and broker a deal. The mediator is paid for their services and recognized by the other parties in their role as facilitator. He/she can come with innovative solutions, and actively lead and influence the process. But, just like the advisor, the mediator needs to gain the confidence of other parties and evoke enthusiasm. A mediator has no formal ownership of the business, but can be given the permission to take decisions by the other partners involved.
3. **Finance investors** are generally initiators of the partnership and members of the partnership. In this matrix, being financial investor means that despite being a shareholder of the business, as a facilitator the investor has no automatic decision-making power. There can be different reasons for this, for example the investor has no seat in the board, or is not the final decision maker in the organization or needs to combine the facilitator role with daily work, which can lead to a loss of momentum.
4. **Active shareholders** differ from finance investors because they have decision power and the mandate to act pro-actively. Active shareholders are fully committed to the partnership and can create momentum. Active shareholders have their own interests and goals and are not objective. Generally the active stakeholder is the initiator of the partnership. Furthermore they have access to more resources, and inside knowledge of the organizations value, culture and procedures.

Depending on the situation, a different type of facilitator is required to broker partnerships that are economically sustainable and pro-poor. In order to understand the role a facilitator can play under different circumstances it is necessary to understand the changing position and responsibilities of the other actors involved in the partnerships, and some of the challenges involved.

Changing position, responsibilities and challenges of actors involved in pro-poor businesses

There are different actors involved in pro-poor businesses, such as private sector, public sector, NGOs and donors. Over the years the roles of these actors and the way they work together have changed. This part of chapter 1 will look at the trends that affected these changes and the results and challenges that follow from this.

Private sector
The private sector groups involved in pro-poor business partnerships are primarily established businesses that buy commodities from small producers in developing countries. In a globalizing world these businesses are confronted with several developments that strongly influence their procurement policies and the relations with their suppliers. Important developments include processes of liberalization, privatization and institutional reforms, resulting in the need for global buyers to take over tasks that were the responsibilities of the state (Humphrey and Schmitz, 2000; 2002).

Another trend is that of intensified competition, which forces companies to become more competitive in a global market (Boomsma 2008). Firms are cutting costs through outsourcing of activities to areas where they can be performed at lower cost and increasing efficiency in the chain. There is also increased competition for natural resources: decades of overexploitation combined with high rates of economic growth in economic powerhouses like China and India make it more difficult to source certain raw materials, such as hard woods, spices, minerals, agricultural commodities and fish. Prices for other resources such as food crops and fuel are rising. This requires companies to identify new supply regions and invest in developing new value chains.

Another trend is more related to the demand side. Consumer tastes and preferences change. For example, people in northern regions have acquired a taste for tropical fruits for which they now expect a year round supply in their local supermarket. This forces companies to look for new production areas that can fill gaps in supply. There are also rising public concerns for social and environmental effects of global business, which results in a growing demand of consumers for quality and traceable products (Boomsma 2008; Heslin and Ochoa 2008) manufactured under appropriate social and environmental conditions.

Increasingly civil society forces companies to take more responsibility for social and environmental issues not only in their own factories but in the whole value chain. In addition to pressure from civil society, ethical motivations from employees and managers within the company are increasingly playing a role. Finally, on a more regional and local level, buyers face increasing risks for supplier failure: for example climate change, political instability, old age of farmers, urban migration of youth have all increased buyers' risks for supplier failure (Laven 2010).

As a result of these developments companies are forced to find the right balance between traceable and quality products, cost effective and efficient value chains, and social and environmental responsibility (Boomsma 2008). Naturally balancing these elements causes conflicts within the company and various actors in the value chain. In their pursuit of sustainable procurement practices the private sector sees itself confronted with several challenges:
- Many businesses are unfamiliar with business practices in developing countries.
- Businesses often lack the capacity to develop the level of skills, management and organization structure and infrastructure at producer level needed to operation the value chain successfully.
- Businesses need to invest in making their current products and value chains more sustainable and in developing and marketing sustainable products. These investments in development can make the end-product uncompetitive on the world market.
- Even companies who invest in producers often find it difficult to create relationships with farmers that result in a stable and reliable supply. Side selling remains an issue.
- The priorities of the private sector are foremost time, profitability and economic performance.
- The private sector tends to be very dynamic and sometimes even chaotic, and priorities can change quickly. Priorities also depend on the manager in place and its motivations and available budget for investments.

Berdegue *et al.* (2008) note that despite these challenges the private sector is very effective in linking smallholders to dynamic markets and building capacity, but this often does not result in lasting economic empowerment of farmers beyond the trade relations. Once the value chain is functioning there is little incentive for companies to invest in further development of smallholders. Therefore it is important that the business sector is receptive to the pro-poor goals of the partnership and is willing to integrate and build capacity in the value chain, through establishing transparent relationships with all actors in the value chain, including small-scale producers.

In establishing relations with the private sector, two issues need to be taken into account. The first issue concerns the interest of the company involved. This interest may range from direct commercial interests to more intangible interests of corporate social responsibility (table 1.1).[1] In this respect important questions are what are the mission, vision and core competencies of the company? What are the expected benefits from the business venture?

Table 1.1. Interest of the private enterprise

Corporate Social Responsibility (CSR) benefits	Commercial benefits
Company reputation	Reduced costs
Improved working environment	Increased quality
Credibility towards opinion- and policymakers	More control over supply chain
Increased knowledge base for internationalization	Entering untapped markets
	Access to public funding
	Branding benefits

The second issue concerns the company's commitment (table 1.2). The commitment of the company may range from hands-on involvement in setting up the venture, to hands-off involvement in providing preconditions. Important questions in this respect are: what are the ongoing programs or business processes that the venture links up with ('institutional buy-in')? How does the firm perceive its role and contributions? Which persons will actively support the venture ('internal champions')?

Table 1.2 Form of commitment by the private enterprise

Hands-off	Hands-on
Loans / investment capital	Operational involvement
Assured market outlet	Staff / expertise
Pre-financing of purchase orders	Resources
Price premium	Joint venture

Based on the company's interests and commitment, there are distinct patterns of private sector engagement with pro-poor business ventures. For example, the private enterprise provides charity funds for the promotion of business ventures in developing countries. The enterprise is not involved in these ventures ('hands-off'), and has no direct commercial interests, but expects to improve its CSR image. Another pattern can be that the private enterprise offers expertise and/or funds to support capacity building of SMEs in developing countries. The enterprise expects CSR benefits rather than direct commercial returns. Another option is that the private enterprise provides a market outlet or investment capital for business ventures in developing

---

[1] Personal communication Lucian Peppelenbos, 2008.

countries. The enterprise is not involved in setting up these ventures ('hands-off'), but expects a beneficial trade relation or return upon investment. Lastly, the private enterprise can have a direct commercial interest in improving its supply relationships with small-scale farmers or distributors. The enterprise commits itself to support and do business with these SMEs.

Producers and local traders
Market liberalization, globalization and the withdrawal of the public sector from markets for agricultural inputs have had far reaching consequences for smallholder farmers. There is no longer a state marketing board which buys from the farmers at a fixed price, but there are multiple traders which offer different prices at different moments. Smallholders now need to compete with their counterparts in other areas of the world. Prices can fluctuate tremendously from year to year, and smallholders need to choose between different traders. Some may offer low prices, but come every year, while others may be opportunists, who only arrive in years of shortages on the world markets and high prices. Some may offer inputs such as seed and fertilizer. Often these inputs are no longer subsidized by the government. Smallholders tend to lack an understanding of how the global, free market works. Together with insecurity over prices and buyers this makes it increasingly difficult to make well-informed decisions over which crops to grow.

Farmer organizations are crucial actors in pro-poor businesses, representing the weakest segment of agricultural market chains, namely the smallholders. The great diversity of farmers' organizations and ways they represent farmers vary per sector, country and even locality. In addition the role of farmer organizations has changed over time. For example in Sub-Saharan Africa the withdrawal of the state from marketing, quality control, price stabilization and many other services has gone hand-in-hand with the reformation of formerly state controlled cooperatives. Just like the private players higher up in the chain, they became responsible for their own management and often privatized (Wennink *et al.* 2007: 27).

In a partnership it is crucial to get to know the farmer organization and to create trust and understanding of each others expectations. As a group the producers also pose serious challenges that need to be addressed when setting up pro-poor partnerships. These challenges include a lack of skills and lack of access to finance and agricultural inputs, which often leads to products of inferior quality. Differences in quality, due to poor quality management systems (or their absence) can also be problematic. Lack of quality management systems and therefore nonuniformity of products between farmers, and even within one batch, increases processing cost (sorting and grading) and complicates marketing. Other issues include:
- Lack of organization, which increases transaction cost for private sector and limits negotiation power.
- Lack of trust amongst farmers themselves and between farmers and traders.
- Limited access to markets.
- Lack of political representation.
- Underdeveloped infrastructure.
- Lack of commitment and opportunistic behaviour.

The result of these issues is that many smallholders and small traders fail to participate in global value chains, and if they do they often only receive small returns.

With respect to the involvement of the producers and small traders we can distinguish two main issues. The first issue concerns the benefits and incentives for the producers and small traders to become involved in the business. Are these based on tangible and visible benefits (such as higher prices or increased volumes of production)? Or are benefits intangible (or more indirect) for example working under better health conditions, consolidation of relationship with buyers? The second issue, already emphasised above, is about the capacity of producers and small traders to become involved in the pro-poor business. Are the producers organized? Do they have access to information, services and training? Is there enough trust to build a long-term relationship?

Public sector
The last two decades have seen the demise of Communism and the entrance of the IMF structural adjustment programs to address the mounting debt from developing countries. Privatisation of state enterprises and market liberalization were amongst the key conditions for IMF and World Bank assistance. As a result of this, planned economies have given way to an economy coordinated by the free market, national marketing boards for commodities such as coffee, tea, and grains have been dismantled, state owned banks privatized, trading and export licenses granted to new private companies, subsidies for agricultural inputs slashed and agricultural extension services dismantled or privatized.

It is often argued that the ability of the public sector and its mandate to make specific pro-poor interventions has been decreased by trade liberalization and structural adjustment. But even in liberalized markets dominated by the private sector, governments can still influence development (Ton *et al*, 2008). Firstly it can enable rural economic growth through infrastructure development, investing in rural education and community development, promotion of competition in supporting sectors such as energy, transport and banking. Secondly it can influence the direction of development, and make it more pro-poor through legislation and subsidies that help small producers; for example by subsidizing extension services to small farmers, encouraging banks to provide loans to small farmers. It can also encourage private sector firms to source from small-scale farmers, providing services such as technical assistance and access to certification schemes and adjust the development of market standards so that the cost of compliance does not lead to widespread exclusion (Berdegue *et al.* 2008). Furthermore it can influence the agricultural sector through taking part in international trade negotiations, and subsidies for inputs.

Another important role of the government is to set the boundaries of the playing field and guard them, i.e. through legislation on working conditions and environmental standards. Although the improvement of conditions, such as infrastructure, import barriers, stimulation of innovation, attracting investment, and education, tend to happen on an industry wide scale, they can be crucial conditions for the success of particular chains. In fact government led interventions in the agricultural sector have been crucial in most countries with successful agricultural sectors (Berdegue *et al.* 2008). There are however many challenges with respect to involvement of the public sector in pro-poor businesses. For example, the government is not automatically a 'neutral enabler', but often represents the interests of certain economic sectors and groups within society, and personal interests are sometimes involved. Secondly the capacities of developing country governments to manage successful interventions that lead to pro-poor agricultural development are generally very limited (Laven, 2010).

NGOs and donors
Non-profit partners tend to act as a kind of watchdog and are generally concerned with issues of exclusion and equity. With the changing role of the public sector, NGOs are now forced to work together with the private sector. There is a trend that non-profit partners look for partnerships with the NGOs. Donor organizations have a role to play in the development of pro-poor business partnerships in situations where essential skills, organization and support services are lacking, and the private and public sector are not willing and/or able to solve these gaps. Through addressing these issues donor organizations and NGOs can make smallholder farmers a more attractive partner for the private sector. Furthermore, through linking farmers with the private sector they can improve their income. For example NGO's can help set-up support services such as training and seed procurement to small businesses that are not yet provided by the market. They can support development of producer organizations, thus increasing their negotiation power and reducing transaction costs for the private sector. Another option is that they can assist them in negotiations with the private and public sector. Through advocacy they can help marginalized groups to defend their rights and gain access to public services.

There are also challenges when dealing with non-profit organizations. First, some organizations are reluctant (or feel uncomfortable) to cooperate directly with the private sector. Such organizations tend to work with producer organizations and public agencies and avoid initiatives in the economic sphere. Second, in situations where civil society organizations are working with the private sector to create poverty alleviation, one of the biggest issues is a lack of understanding and experience of business economics, business culture and specific sectors. This is reflected in issues that make their interventions less effective, such as:
- Automatically selecting the level of farmers as an entry point for interventions.
- Product oriented in stead of market oriented projects where markets and consumer demand are not properly analysed. This leads to the production of products for which there is no consumer demand, or operations that lack the essential marketing strategies and skills.
- Disregard of the fact that value chains cannot be built by outside agents but must be built around private sector initiatives (Berdegué et al. 2008).
- A disregard for the fact that value chains are composed of many specialized companies rather than one company which is in charge of everything (Berdegué et al. 2008).
- Unrealistic expectations towards businesses, for instance about their support towards smallholders in providing training and investments in the partnerships. But also about the prices that businesses can pay. In commodity markets, global market prices have to be followed in order to remain competitive. When global market prices drop, businesses have to follow these trends.
- Unsustainable donations or funding with insufficient conditions attached and without an exit strategy for donor support. They can create a hand-out culture where people expect gifts and are not willing to deliver results. Another situation to avoid is market distortion.

Tensions between different actors
The different interests of all actors and the challenges they face, can cause tensions between the different groups. It is the task of the partnership facilitator to spot, understand and adequately deal with these tensions.

For example, conflict arises between producer groups and business when relationships move from a spot market to an integrated value chain, where relationships are structured around prices. Apart from the height of the price and the time of payment, which is often a crucial issue for smallholders, price agreements can be a source of conflict leading to dissatisfaction. As a result it can be difficult to prevent producers from selling to other companies (e.g. the ginger case). On the other hand, price agreements can lead to more stable income for producers. The challenge is to construct a proper incentive structure, both for producers and for private partners, to keep them committed to the partnership (e.g. the jatropha case). Timely supply and delivering the required quality are other important challenges.

There can be also important tensions between the private sector and the non-profit sector. For example there can be a tension between the commercial interest of a company and the social and political agenda of a non-profit actor (e.g. the tuna case). A company's starting point is often a commercially profitable venture. The starting point of NGO's and donors tends to be exactly the opposite: the goal is poverty alleviation, and as little as possible should end up in the form of company profits or salaries. Conflicts can arise if for example the non-profit sector wants to include the poorest and smallest farmers in a project to maximize the poverty alleviation potential, whereas the private sector picks the best skilled and largest farmers to maximize the chance of commercial success. A second conflict source involves information use. Whereas knowledge institutes want to publish detailed accounts of projects, the private sector is reluctant to release figures that can be used by competitors (e.g. the cocoa case).

Tensions between producers and the non-profit sector are also common. These tensions are mainly based on unrealistic assumptions on the ability of the producer-organization to represent its members' interests and on the commitment of farmers to the organization of which they have become a member. There are also assumptions about the ability of producer organization to get involved in marketing, processing and/or trading issues. Cutting out the small traders is an often used solution for inequalities in the chain, neglecting the role these middlemen play. Tensions can also arise because of unrealistic estimates about volume of production and trade (e.g. ginger case).

One of the major tasks of the facilitator is to spot, understand and adequately deal with these tensions. Over the years KIT has performed different types of facilitating roles, this bulletin shares these experiences.

2 Bridging business and development – in practice

This chapter presents five cases of pro-poor business engineering in which KIT plays the role of facilitator, albeit in different forms.

Case 1. Sourcing ginger from Sierra Leone shows how KIT was involved as an advisor, bringing in a local ginger enterprise as potential business partners for Unifine Sauces and Spices.

Case 2. Supporting sustainable tuna fishing in Ghana tells how KIT facilitated as an advisor a Ghanaian public-private partnership for sustainable tuna fisheries

Case 3. Organic Cocoa Dominican Republic S.A. describes how KIT became involved as finance-investor in an organic cocoa factory in the Dominican Republic.

Case 4. Processing biodiesel from jatropha with smallholders in Mali is about the experience of KIT as an active shareholder in Mali Biocarburant SA.

Case 5 Yiriwa S.A.: Setting up a trade house for organic products made in Mali shows KIT's involvement as active shareholder in a trading company of cotton, sesame and soya bean.

Case 1. Sourcing ginger from Sierra Leone: no success without transparency and communication.[2]

By Marije Boomsma

Introduction

Unifine Sauces and Spices sources a wide range of spices from all over the world for its sauces, dressings, spices and seasonings. In August 2005 Unifine approached KIT with a request to offer support for changing its procurement strategy. Unifine wanted to switch from sourcing through traders and brokers to direct contracts with reliable spice producers in developing countries. The driving factor was Unifine's need for better quality assurance and full traceability in the supply chain, as well as the diversification of suppliers. KIT regarded this request as a challenge to match Unifine's business interests with KIT's mission of sustainable poverty alleviation and promotion of sustainable purchasing. Through Cordaid KIT successfully identified the Cotton Tree Foundation Ginger Enterprise (CTFGE) in Sierra Leone as a potential producer of ginger. This case describes KIT's experiences in the role of an advisor that has difficulties in creating transparency in setting up chain partnerships.

Reviving the ginger industry

After the initial contact, Unifine shared a list of twenty priority spices with indicative volumes and prices, whereupon KIT activated its network to identify business opportunities. Because of its poverty alleviation agenda all the suppliers identified by KIT were organizations of small-scale farmers, or processors working with small-scale farmers in a way that was beneficial for farmers and economically and socially sustainable. However, the partner search proved to be challenging, because at the time few of KIT's partners were involved in trade and commerce. Despite a large partner search through KIT's extensive network only three opportunities were identified:
- Dried ginger from Sierra Leone;
- Paprika powder from Malawi and Chile;
- Lemon grass from Sri Lanka.

The first opportunity proved to be the most promising. Sierra Leone has been growing ginger since the eighteenth century when colonial traders introduced it from Asia. At the time the

---

[2] This business case is written down by KIT and therefore reflects on KIT's experience only. As a consequence the conclusions of this Chapter may not always be shared by all partners of this business case.

crop was dried and exported for the pharmaceutical and confectionary industry. In the nineteen seventies Sierra Leone became the third largest producer of ginger, after India and Jamaica. Unfortunately, Sierra Leone lost its market position in the eighties, when the world market price for ginger dropped and farmers shifted their production to other crops.

After the war, in 2003, a Chinese supported project in central Sierra Leone brought in 53 tons of fresh ginger from China in order to revitalize the industry and take advantage of the growing demand for ginger in Europe and the United States. Unfortunately the Chinese ginger variety grew poorly on Sierra Leone's soils. The resulting crop proved to be too spicy and oily for consumption.

At that stage the Cotton Tree Foundation (CTF) (see box 2.1 Business Actors) began promoting planting of the original varieties of ginger among small-holder farmers in the north-east of the country, where few other cash-crops are produced. Cordaid, a Dutch donor organization, supported the ginger project of CTF with a grant total of 150,000 USD. The project lasted from 2003 to 2006 and trained 1,231 ginger growers.

Towards the end of this project Cordaid agreed to assist the Cotton Tree Foundation with commercializing their ginger project. By then, KIT had introduced Unifine to Cordaid. First, the Foundation sent samples of dried ginger to Unifine in The Netherlands. Once these samples passed Unifine's quality standards, CTF became serious in setting up a ginger processing and export enterprise in Sierra Leone. At the end of 2006, with support from Cordaid, a new venture was launched called the Cotton Tree Foundation Ginger Enterprise (CTFGE).

While the opportunity existed for a commercial venture between CTFGE and Unifine, there were major differences in their history and capabilities. CFTGE is a newly-formed company in an economically depressed region (still recovering from a devastating civil war), Unifine is a leader in the European spice trade. A facilitator – such as KIT – was needed to help bridge the gap.

In February 2007, Unifine planned a visit to CTFGE in Sierra Leone in order to audit the company's business processes and supply relations, and to agree/negotiate an informal chain partnership agreement between supplier and buyer. KIT decided to join Unifine on its own expense, as part of a larger program on sustainable procurement, to ensure that a sustainable business deal would be set up that could be the start of a longer term supply chain partnership between Unifine and CTFGE.

During the visit Unifine provided technical advice, provided the CTFGE with a technical handbook for the production of ginger, and conducted a standard audit. This audit included raw materials, quality, hygiene, processing, and management skills. As part of this audit the processing plants, where ginger is cleaned, cut and dried, were visited. The outcome of the audit was sufficiently positive: although the facilities and quality systems of CTFGE had major limitations, particularly with regards to logistics, the ginger was meeting quality standards and as a result, Unifine agreed to make an order for 2007.

CTFGE wanted to supply a total amount of 140 tons dried ginger to Unifine and in order to do so, Cordaid provided a short term 6-month loan of 85,100 USD.

> **Box 2.1. Business Actors**
>
> **Unifine**
> Unifine develops, produces and delivers sauces and spices for the foodservice, meat-packing and food industry. It sources 500 tons ginger on an annual basis and sells it at the European market. In this case Unifine is the buyer of the ginger from Sierra Leone.
>
> **Cotton Tree Foundation Ginger Enterprise (CTFGE)**
> CTFGE, a ginger processing and exporting company with three processing plants in Northwestern Sierra Leone employing 100 female part time workers and approximately 15 full time workers.
>
> **Farmers**
> Approximately 400-500 farmers (before subsistence farmers) producing and supplying ginger for CTFGE. Place: near processing plants CTFGE.
>
> **Cotton Tree Foundation (CTF)**
> CTF is an NGO in Sierra Leone that works to improve the welfare of people, families and communities through agricultural development. CTF has set up CTFGE.
>
> **Cordaid**
> Cordaid, a Dutch development organization with expertise in emergency aid and structural poverty eradication. Cordaid assisted CTF with commercializing their ginger project.
>
> **KIT**
> KIT played the role as advisor and identified the CTFGE as potential business partner for Unifine.

However, an analysis from KIT showed that the production and organizational capacity of the enterprise was still far too limited to complete an order of this size. Firstly, good management was not yet in place. The company was run by the Foundation which was making all business decisions, for instance where the processing plants were located (which were too far from each other and therefore causing high transport costs). Furthermore, staff members were being paid by the Foundation and financial administration was still lacking. Therefore the revenues, cost, profit and losses as well as the required working capital were unknown. Furthermore, according to KIT's calculations, the business was currently not profitable and would need to trade at least 100 tons of ginger to break even. In addition, it became clear that the managing director was planning to leave the company. Finally, the farmers that were supplying the company were not yet identified.

With these limitations in mind, KIT advised both parties to lower the order from 140 to at most 80 tons of ginger for 2007. At the end of the visit the agreement was therefore reached that CTFGE would supply Unifine with 80 tons of ginger between March and May 2007. Furthermore Unifine would pay a 50 USD price premium per ton on top of the world market price to finance the development of the new business. CTFGE on the other hand promised to formulate a proper business plan and to identify the farmers in the supply chain through a farmers survey. Under the guidance of KIT the partners signed a partnership agreement including the vision, roles, volumes, price, quality, contract conditions, exclusivity and communication, in order to ratify the promises made.

KIT proposed to CTFGE and Cordaid to facilitate the process of drawing up a business plan and conducting a farmer's survey. This proposal offer was, however, rejected by Cordaid and was taken up by Cordaid's in-house consultant IC Consult. During the remainder of the partnership, the communication between the different partners was problematic and information was not being shared.

During March and May, Unifine contacted CTFGE several times through email and phone in order to be informed about the progress of harvesting and processing, often without success. In fact, later during the season, Unifine discovered that the managing director had quit his job. Still CTFGE ensured that everything would work out according to plan and that a new director would be hired, but at the end of the season the actual volume that was produced turned out to be only 40 tons instead of the promised 80 tons. The reason that was given by CTFGE was that the rainy season had come too early and had disrupted drying the fresh ginger during June. Furthermore, the new director had not yet been recruited. In August/September the Foundation conducted a survey that identified about 450 farmers. The outcomes of the study were not shared with the other partners.

For Unifine not fulfilling the order could have been a disaster, because it had to fulfill contracts with its buyers in Europe. Fortunately, Unifine was able to buy the remaining 40 tons of ginger on the spot market at a reasonable price, and it did not incur great losses.

In November of 2007, the director and the financial manager of the Cotton Tree Foundation visited the Netherlands. Unifine and KIT were invited to a briefing in which the production season of 2007 was evaluated. The actual versus potential production volume was still unclear at that time as well as the number of farmers and the absence of a managing director. The missing communication between CTFGE and Unifine was discussed. KIT and Unifine stressed that a proper partnership should be open, transparent and trustful.

In spite of early disappointments, Unifine was still committed to its goal to diversify the source of ginger and wished to continue building the partnership. A new agreement was reached between the parties for the 2008 season that included:
- A new order from Unifine for a minimum of 40 tons of dried ginger, with an option to procure a maximum of 75 tons at a world market price;
- A promise from CTFGE to hire a new managing director in December 2007 - the new MD would be responsible for improved communications, especially on crucial problems such as lower than planned production volumes;
- A Cordaid promise to continue support to CTF and CTFGE: Cordaid would provide a grant of 100,000 USD for training, investments in hardware (mainly logistics and working capital).

Unifine stressed that only world market prices could be paid for the ginger (approximately 1400 Euro per ton at that time) and that as far as they are concerned this meant that CTFGE should develop into a commercial business that had to sell ginger at competitive prices.

After this meeting CTF hired a new managing director, but communication did not truly improve. In April 2008 Unifine began requesting information about production progress. CTFGE replied that 10 tons had been shipped in early May. However, by mid June that container still had not arrived and there was no sign of the remaining 30 tons being delivered. A further explanation came later that local market prices for ginger had almost doubled, due to the rising demand from Guinea and local beer factories. CTFGE could therefore not afford to buy more than 10 tons at the price agreed to with Unifine.

Despite the difficulties between Unifine and CTFG, to date Unifine is still interested in sourcing ginger from Sierra Leone. Unfortunately CTFGE keeps on being silent. The latest development in the spice industry is the ambition of the Dutch spice sector to make their supply chains more sustainable. Unifine (now Intertaste)[3] is a very active player in this process.

Need for a full mandate

KIT was involved as a mediator in setting up the partnership of Unifine and CTFGE, but only during the early beginning of the process. Despite KIT's ambitions, this role stopped after the first field trip. Since then KIT has been on the side-line serving as an advisor to Unifine.

KIT wanted to play a mediation role in setting up a sustainable and pro-poor value chain, but its expectations were unfounded. KIT's role as mediator was hog-tied because it lacked the full mandate to intervene. KIT was never formally contracted by all of the partners for this role; this was an initiative of the buyer. As a result our efforts remained a stand-alone activity on behalf of Unifine that was looking for new sourcing markets. The other partners were occupied with setting up a production and trading company in a post-war environment that was in fact not yet ready for export, even though the supplier thought it was. The two sides operated more or less independently at different speed levels.

Inclusion of small producers

KIT missed the opportunity to truly influence this case and help to establish a new pro-poor business, when it was unable to broker a more turn-key position with the main donor – Cordaid and its overseas client CTF. As a result, KIT was powerless to advocate for including ginger farmers in the value chain partnership and to actively support farmers in this. For Unifine and KIT it remains questionable whether farmers were actually committed to supply their ginger to CTFGE or whether they had other, better marketing channels.

All actors (buyers, suppliers, investors, support agencies, small-scale producers) must be included in the design of the partnership to streamline expectations and to ensure commitment. Buyers need to be able to trace their products back to farm level and therefore they need to directly communicate with farmers. If small scale producers are not involved, the supply chain will have too many weak links and be likely to break down, as was the case in 2008. Inclusion of the farmers was probably the most crucial measure to make this venture work, and a key reason for its failure.

---

[3] In 2008 Unifine was sold. The new name of the company is Intertaste.

Communication and leadership is to be blamed

In this case there has been a critical lack of communication between the supplier (CTFGE) and donor agency (Cordaid) on one side, and the buyer (Unifine) and KIT on the other side. Communication about, amongst others expectations and realistic goal setting for production and export targets, did not come of the ground. This has hold down the overall process. As a consequence partners lost an eye for what once linked them all together, which was their common goal of setting up a sustainable ginger value chain.

The lack of communication and collaboration between all stakeholders from an early stage – and the inability to overcome this challenge – was another cause of frustration in the Sierra Leone ginger value chain. Unfortunately nor KIT nor another partner did manage to lead this process in the right direction.

The future

It is now three years since the project started and a lot has been learned about sustainable business in that time. KIT is still involved in the spice sector and part of the process to make the sector more sustainable. Moreover, communication with the Sierra Leone partners is still ongoing. There is an ongoing interest in making ginger trade from Sierra Leone work, which is a hopeful sign for the future. To revive this project we have learned that the next step would be to get all partners together and to agree upon sustainable ambitions, roles and responsibilities. Foremost, a realistic long term path that leads to sustainable growth needs to be established.

Case 2. Supporting sustainable tuna fishing in Ghana

By Bart de Steenhuijsen-Piters

Introduction

Fishing communities along Ghana's coast generally live in poverty, but Ghana has vast resources of deep-sea fish that remain out of reach of these communities. Sustainably caught tuna fetches high international market prices and might contribute to improving livelihoods if a well-organized pro-poor business is set up. In order to realize this opportunity a public-private partnership has been established with the help of KIT. The partnership joins hands between Dutch fish traders, Philippine boat builders, Ghanaian businessmen and fishing communities, as well as the governments of Ghana and the Netherlands. This case highlights KIT's efforts to facilitate the business development/creation process in this virtual forest of divergent interests, unequal access to assets and different cultures. KIT's role was to bring order in this complexity and guide partners through a process that resulted in a transparent fishing business that involves less-endowed communities in decision taking and stimulates pro-poor economic growth.

The fresh tuna business is booming and supply cannot meet demand. Fresh tuna has partially replaced wild salmon which has become too scarce due to overexploitation. Current world market prices for fresh tuna range from 15 to18 US$ per kg of fresh loin. Global tuna populations are threatened by large-scale factory fishing operations that process fresh fish into canned tuna. Canning converts a high value product into a low-value product because of its long shelf life and global commodity marketing. World wholesale prices for canned tuna do not exceed 5 US$ per kg. There is increasing public concern over the sustainability of the large-scale fishing sector, notably tuna fishing.

Two million people in Ghana derive their livelihoods directly or indirectly from open sea fishing. Most of the fishing activities take place in inshore waters due to a lack of seaworthy fishing boats, equipment and expertise. However, some Ghanaian fishermen also temporarily migrate to foreign waters to catch fish. Those people who depend on inshore fishing are affected by over-fishing resulting in small catches and significant poverty. These fishermen use dugout canoes. Cutting timber for making the canoes has recently been banned for reasons of forest conservation, increasing the price of the canoes and negatively affecting people's livelihoods.

Starting a new partnership

The Dutch – Ghanaian public-private partnership (PPP) for sustainable tuna fisheries hopes to solve the main chronic problems affecting the fishing communities of Ghana. Its major goals are to establish a value chain for fresh tuna that involves local fishermen, improves their incomes, and reduces the pressure on inshore fish populations. A new, more sustainable mode of deep-sea fishing with new fiberglass boats will be introduced. Two inter-related ventures have been established to achieve these goals: a shipyard to locally build fiberglass boats and a fishing operation that coordinates the tuna marketing - from the Ghanaian fishermen catch to sale by Dutch traders on the world market. Glass fiber construction technology and training will be provided through a Philippine partner (see box 2.2). Fishermen will be paid a fair price that will significantly increase their income. Credit facilities and shareholding are among the instruments to increase involvement of small-scale fishermen.

The partnership received euro 900,000 in public funding from the Dutch Ministry of Foreign Affairs. Business associates from Ghana, the Netherlands and Philippines also contributed euro 700,000 private equity providing these investors with shares in the two joint ventures.

Box 2.2. Main actors in the Public-Private Partnership

Rainbow Fish consultants. Dutch consultancy firm that initiated the programme, shareholder in both joint ventures

DaySeaDay BV and van Wijk BV. Dutch fish traders who will market the tuna in Europe and who are shareholders in both joint ventures

Phineghan Ltd. A new joint venture in Ghana for sustainable tuna fisheries

Fine Marine Ltd. A new joint venture in Ghana for building fiberglass boats

Dolphin Shipping Services Ltd. and Inter-Seas Fisheries Ltd. Companies belonging to Ghanaian business man/investor, shareholder in both joint ventures, managing director of Phineghan Ltd.

The Ghana National Canoe Fishermen Council (GCFC) represents 100,000 canoe fishermen. GCFC is a potential shareholder in Phineghan Ltd. The Ghana Inshore Fishermen Association (GIFA) represents the semi-industrial fishing industry And represents approximately 5000 members. GIFA is also potential shareholder in Phineghan Ltd.

Gratis Foundation. Ghanaian NGO, shareholder and managing director in Fine Marine Ltd.

KIT. Dutch knowledge institute, facilitator of the programme

Stoneworks, a Philippine fiberglass boat builder, shareholder in Fine Marine Ltd.

Exploratory stage

In 2002 the owner of DaySeaDay, a Dutch market leader in fresh fish, met a Ghanaian trader who told him about the vast fish resources of Ghana. Intrigued by this information, the CEO sent his son, working in his company, to Ghana to explore the potential for sourcing fresh tuna. After meeting with the Ghanaian fishermen it was clear that tuna is available in abundance, but that the fishing industry was not well developed. Thousands of small-scale fishermen were landing undersized, juvenile fish while a fleet of foreign vessels provided the canning industry with frozen tuna. In Ghana there was no processing of fresh fish for export, nor was there a cold chain facility to preserve fresh fish for safe local consumption.

Following this first visit, an experienced fish-trading consultant was hired to help prepare a plan for the procurement of fresh tuna from Ghana. They traveled a second time to Ghana to further explore the bottlenecks to establishing a cold-storage facility and look for local business partners.

In 2005 a funding proposal was developed with the help of KIT and submitted to the Dutch Directorate-General for International Cooperation (DGIS) that had just launched its call for Public Private Partnerships.

An inception phase (2006) was proposed to put the partnership on the ground and achieve some critical agreements, resulting in a clear go/no go decision moment. DGIS adopted this recommendation and gave the green light for elaborating detailed work plans and a full partnership agreement, not only engaging private sector, but also the Governments of Ghana and the Netherlands. At that moment, almost four years had passed since the owner of DaySeaDay met his Ghanaian friend at the Costa del Sol.

The inception phase started in April 2006 and was concluded by November the same year when eleven partner representatives signed the partnership agreement, upon which two joint ventures – one for fisheries and another one for building glassfibre boats – were registered. In this phase several new constraints had to be addressed. Among them were:
- Hostility or mistrust from the fishermen who had bad experiences with foreign aid and could not distinguish the fresh tuna business proposal from previous donor projects.
- Inadequate organization of the Ghana Inshore Fishermen Association that allowed concentration of power in the hands of its chairman.
- Annoyance by the Ghanaian businessmen with the attitude of the canoe fishermen. It took some time before the fishermen understood that this was not a project based on subsidies, but business to business. Initially the local businessmen did not see the importance of shareholding by the fishermen associations and strongly advocated for a 'nothing for free' policy. Shareholding by fishermen associations was agreed, provided that they invested equity capital. Social capital in the form of community mobilization for the project was not considered an asset worth shares.
- General mistrust about budget allocations. There was no prior agreement among partners to early budget spending, fees and ways to recover these costs.
- The Government of Ghana was supportive but continued a laissez-faire policy towards regulating fisheries, allowing all parties to continue their fishing operations as usual. For example, the Minister approved licenses for more then 40 fishing trawlers owned by Asian-Ghanaian joint ventures in the same period that this initiative for sustainable fisheries was launched.
- Although all partners committed to invest capital and arrange for making a first installment, in practice several partners did not transfer the agreed amount. This increased mistrust instead of building confidence.

During the first months after the inception phase Gratis Foundation withdrew as investor and proposed to make available a site that is owned by this NGO for the shipyard for which shares would be provided in return. The Ghanaian fish exporter, an expected investor, experienced serious liquidity problems. Philippine parties did not transfer any capital to the joint venture account.

DGIS proposed that a local process facilitator be identified and hired to act as local moderator between parties. The facilitator is locally contracted and backed up by KIT. DGIS also contracted with PriceWaterhouseCoopers to provide auditing services and financial reporting capacity to the Partnership. Both services provided greater transparency at a stage when mutual trust was needed to strengthen the partnership.

The collaboration between commercial parties and small-scale fishermen was mainly a result of pressure by KIT. The fresh tuna venture could have been established more easily without the involvement of independent small-scale fishermen and their association. The original idea was to finance one big fleet owned by the joint venture, then to recruit fishermen on a contractual basis. The fishermen associations were initially not included as potential co-owners and KIT worked hard to include them in the negotiation process.

The local facilitator improved the communication between the many partners, working in a participatory manner and drawing up formal service contracts between the joint venture and the fishing associations and organizing a stakeholder workshop for Ghanaian partners. Nevertheless, the Fishing associations remain skeptical about the merits of the PPP and are not convinced that benefits from the two joint ventures will be equally shared. The Fishing associations are at this stage still discussing with their members the option of becoming shareholder through equity investment. This being completely novel to them, they also meet hostility. This principle is rather important and should be carefully dealt with. The partnership must provide factual and tangible evidence of its goal to benefit fishermen too.

Monitoring and evaluation of progress (a requirement of the DGIS support) will be carried out by PWC and through bi-annual reporting by the project leader. The establishment of a monitoring system and feedback structure proposed by KIT, has only been supported by the local facilitator. The idea of improving operations through monitoring performance is new/foreign to all other parties. Such a position also presents a challenge in gaining support from partners on addressing policy issues that promote sustainable fisheries management.

The next table gives an overview of stages, poverty indicators and roles of KIT.

Table 2.1 Overview of stages, poverty indicators and roles of KIT

Stage	Indicator of pro-poor relevance	Role of KIT
Idea 2005	The business idea was not explicitly pro-poor, but would generate foreign exchange and employment to Ghana	None
Proposal development for DGIS supported PPP 2005/early 2006	• Include associations of fishermen, notably small scale fishermen • Fix a minimum procurement price of fresh tuna at 1.5 US$/kg • Include associations as optional shareholders • Include costs of capacity development • Include a credit facility to improve access to vessels by small fishermen	Directly included in proposal and actively negotiated in its development. KIT's role was one of advocacy, process facilitation and providing expertise in terms of PPP design

Stage	Indicator of pro-poor relevance	Role of KIT
Inception phase 2006	• Associations and NGO included in the signing of the partnership agreement • Roles of the associations were well communicated and given proper attention • Shareholding by associations remained an option, but not supported (yet) by a credit facility • Steps taken to develop a credit scheme for the procurement of vessels by all fishermen • Dutch investors insist on 'fair price' deal with fishermen	Multiple roles: at times acted on behalf of DGIS, backstopped Ghanaian parties or reported to all stakeholders to maintain transparency
Execution 2007 - date	• Insist who? on the inclusion of small fishermen in first training badge to visit the Philippines • Major attention for the establishment of a credit scheme • Attention for a capacity development and organizational strengthening plan of the fishermen associations • Introduction of fishermen associations as shareholders	Provides focused input in the work plan enhancing inclusion of small fishermen. Overall process is being 'watched' by KIT and engagements are carefully followed

KIT's evolving roles

KIT's role gradually changed from pro-poor business plan designer to partnership facilitator and capacity developer. KIT's first role was solicited by the consultant and DGIS because of its neutrality, independence and reputation as expert in starting pro-poor business ventures and public-private cooperation. This advisory role changed into one of service delivery in terms of capacity development and process facilitation. KIT was however not mandated to actively intervene in times of conflicting interests and slowing down of progress. KIT was also not involved in all internal issues taking place within the two joint ventures.

Active participation in a Public Private Partnership (PPP) results in knowledge generation that is sometimes innovative and unique in the sense that it provides a glance in the 'black box' of private affairs. It should be considered as a form of action research. However, if that is the case, then a much better elaborated learning structure or research design is needed to make full use of all information and data collected.

Over time the role of KIT changed from bridge to the public sector and providing expertise in PPP design, to process facilitator during the inception phase and service provider with well-defined outputs during the implementation phase. Into the future, KIT will negotiate the role of ongoing monitoring and evaluation and creating ownership for a process of learning among some partners. The changing role of KIT may have confused some parties in the PPP and could lead to unrealistic or implicit expectations that are difficult to meet. One conclusion from this experience is that by not being a shareholder (with the resulting vested interests), KIT had to readjust its role to changing circumstances and continuously explain our presence among commercial parties. In the sustainable tuna PPP there was no unconditional and unanimous need among partners for engaging (contracting) KIT as a process facilitator for the entire pilot phase. One of the primary reasons that KIT participates was to mobilize public funds and partially use these funds for enhancing poverty impacts.

There is tension between KIT's role as neutral and independent facilitator and our explicit mission to enhance pro-poor impacts of private business. In fact, KIT cannot claim to be neutral to all parties involved. In the sustainable tuna PPP KIT strongly advocated for small fisherman's' interests, which opposed the interests of businessmen. At other occasions KIT played a more general process facilitation role, while at times we helped local players in their negotiations. This tension between goals and interests and KIT's formal position in such a multi-interest environment needs more attention.

The opportunity to build in pro-poor impacts is greatest in the early phases of the partnership, when the goals, rules and roles are being defined. After that, it is a matter of implementation and supervision that all partners keep their promises and follow the rules set. This is contrary to the typical approach whereby a more long-term informal process is followed and parties establish relationships while doing business. Early agreement on how to achieve poverty impacts is needed, especially if some partners do not fully support such a goal. In such a case, poverty impacts require specific negotiation, because budget funds and efforts are needed that could also be used for other purposes. This implies that, before everything, KIT needs to create a foundation for its involvement – whether short or long-term. Secondly, KIT needs to identify stakeholder groups qualified to represent the poor and become a close/trusted ally to such groups. Only then can KIT get involved in negotiations and act on behalf of the wider community.

Pro-poor impact – more potential than facts so far

The beneficiaries in terms of pro-poor impact are the crews and their families within the community of canoe fishermen. At present, this group represents > 6000 fishermen and over 30,000 people. The tuna PPP is still a pilot activity that has limited immediate impacts, but high potential impacts on poverty through scaling up in the next operational phase. Direct impact will be monitored/measured by KIT based on such criteria as: the income earned by canoe fishermen that participate in a credit facility to procure a vessel and join the tuna fleet. Income will be shared through a custodian system that dictates the division of benefits.

Other impacts related to poverty alleviation include capacity development of the fishermen associations and their active involvement in the governance of the joint ventures. Jobs will be created by the new shipyard venture that is going to build cheap boats designed for small fishing crews. The process of inclusion of small fishermen is binding, once the pilot phase has concluded successfully and formal agreements are in place, the associations are fully involved and informed of added value and world market prices.

To summarize: the most tangible pro-poor impacts so far are:
1 Contracting of a neutral, Ghanaian process facilitator who worked to include the canoe fishermen at critical stages in the negotiation process.
2 Shared power and transparency (in contrast to the initial design where most power was in few hands).

3 Training for capacity development.
4 Shareholding by fishermen associations.
5 Job opportunities at the shipyard
6 A euro 100,000 revolving procurement fund for small-scale fishermen to buy new vessels.
7 An accessible credit facility designed for small fishermen.

The 'proof of the pudding' of improved livelihoods will begin to show once this pilot activity grows in scale and includes larger numbers of fishermen. Real impact can only be measured in terms of enhanced income generation and distribution, levels or organization, negotiation capacity and participation in decision-making processes. These impacts should also sustain themselves over time.

Achieving transparency

Matching public and private goals in a business operation requires resolving intrinsic conflicts of interest. It is more rule than exception that parties initially agree on general objectives, but then divert from collective ground into personal interests. Combining public funding and private finance often results in ad hoc negotiations between parties that do not result in the best use of financial resources. This risk is greater when the financial manager has commercial interests himself and has a degree of freedom to disburse funds. One way to avoid this scenario is to outsource financial management, as it was done in this case to PWC.

Regular monitoring and evaluation, as well as writing circulation of progress reports amongst all partners, enhances transparency and building up trust and confidence. Yet, in order to achieve transparent governing structures, early management of diverging interests and potential conflicts needs great attention.

Business people have little patience for numerous and time consuming formalities and meetings before taking action. However, when initiating a new business – such as the sustainable tuna fishing partnership - that ultimately reduces poverty and for which public funds are mobilized, much more attention must be given to establishing good governance. Pro-poor business engineering is a skill that must be part of early stages of business development. For the tuna fishermen of Ghana achieving a more secure future for themselves and their families may depend on their faith in and the durability of the business structures that have been built during this pilot initiative.

Case 3. Organic Cocoa Dominican Republic S.A.

By Maurits de Koning and Anna Laven

Introduction

Organic cocoa is a booming, demand-driven market, limited only by the shortage of supply of organic raw materials. In the beginning of 2006, Tradin, a trader of organic products, proposed Conacado to jointly buy a cocoa processing factory in the Dominican Republic. Tradin took this initiative to secure supply of organic cocoa and its derivates. Tradin and Conacado have been business partners for about 15 years. KIT became involved in October 2006 by invitation of Tradin in order to facilitate the joint venture.

During a mission to Ethiopia in September 2006 KIT became acquainted with Tradin, a trader of organic products. KIT and Tradin had a similar interest in setting up business projects in developing countries, for Tradin to secure a traceable source of high-quality raw material and for KIT to link local smallholder producers to high-value international markets. It was agreed that cooperation would be explored through a pilot business case, this became a cocoa processing factory in the Dominican Republic together with Conacado, the National Confederation of Dominican Cocoa Producers (see Box 2.3).

> **Box 2.3. 'The first 100% organic cocoa processing factory in the world'**
>
> The business opportunity was setting up the first 100% organic cocoa processing factory in the world, based in San Francisco de Macoris, Dominican Republic. It would produce organic cocoa derivatives for the international market, principally the USA and Europe. The company would be a joint venture between Conacado, Tradin Organic Corporation and KIT Holding B.V under the name Organic Cocoa Dominican Republic S.A. The plant would process up to 5,632 tons per year and would have an estimated turnover of $18 million.

The start-up process

In December 2006, KIT and Tradin presented the pilot business case to KIT management board, the Dutch Railway Pension Fund (SPF) and the Dutch bank ABN-AMRO. The original idea was to buy a cocoa factory that was for sale at the time. Conacado would supply high quality organic cocoa beans to the factory and Tradin would promote and sell the organic cocoa products (cocoa butter, liquor, powder and cocoa cake) in the global market.

Initially KIT was supposed to be an advisor and mediator, advising on project implementation, capacity-building, reporting, and monitoring impacts. Additionally, KIT was seen as the gateway to donor funding, investor capital and low-interest loans. SPF was the capital provider and ABN AMRO was responsible for the financial expertise. In terms of ownership Tradin and Conacado would split the shares, both having 50%. As the cocoa factory was for sale and it was required to take action quickly, KIT, SPF and ABN-AMRO decided to proceed.

The first stage in the business process was to write a sustainable business plan. KIT, together with Tradin, visited the Dominican Republic to jointly do a supply chain analysis, to appraise Conacado and to negotiate with the current owners of the factory.

Box 2.4. Business actors

Conacado (National Confederation of Dominican Cocoa Producers)
Conacado is the world's prime producer of organically certified cocoa beans. In 2006 this farmer organization exported over 20,000 tons of organic cocoa beans. The main role for Conacado in this partnership was the production of organic cocoa beans, which fetch a higher price on the world market than conventional cocoa.

Tradin Organic Corporation B.V. (TOC)
Tradin is TOC's main daughter and a world-leading trading company in organic commodities and derivatives, based in Amsterdam. In the business, Tradin will buy the organic cocoa products which are processed in the Dominican factory. For Tradin a main interest, as a large shareholder, is to secure a traceable source of high quality raw material.

KIT Holding B.V.
KIT was initially asked to play a role as advisor in this pro-poor business. Later KIT was asked to step in as financer-investor. The main interest for KIT in this project was the setting up of a business in the South and to link smallholder producers to a high-value international market. In 2006 the KIT Holding B.V. was established. It holds the group of companies: KIT Publishers B.V., KIT Hotel B.V. and a 40% share in Mali BioCarburant SA (see Case 4).

Besides the three business partners mentioned above, three other stakeholders were involved. Two of them from the early beginning and invited by KIT: SPF as capital provider and ABN-AMRO for their financial expertise. After a couple months ABN-AMRO stepped out and Rabobank International came in.

Before leaving for the Dominican Republic, KIT collected information on Conacado (the Dominican partner) through Tradin and through internet research. KIT did not do a thorough screening of the partner, nor did KIT communicate with Conacado directly. KIT more or less assumed that Conacado was a committed partner, having been a business partner of Tradin for 15 years.

The relationship between Tradin and Conacado got off to a shaky start on the first day of the assessment tour, when Tradin and KIT visited Conacado. Tradin unexpectedly proposed to Conacado to become a minority shareholder of the business with 49% of the shares. Conacado refused the offer on the grounds that they did not want Tradin to have the majority of the shares. In order to prevent an impasse, Tradin and Conacado approached KIT to become a third (minority) shareholder to balance decision making. KIT would step in with 4% of the total shares. For Tradin it was important that there was still a Dutch majority of the shares. Including KIT as a minority shareholder was also desirable to ensure good administrative practices, corporate social responsibility and smooth arbitration of possible conflicts. In addition KIT would provide advisory support in project implementation, capacity-building, reporting, and monitoring of impacts. KIT was also seen as the gateway to donor funding.

In the business each shareholder was supposed to provide a board member for the joint venture. Tradin was taking the lead in recruiting the management. An external advisor, selected by Tradin, would play an important role in all crucial (technical and extension) decision-making. Professionals from outside the Dominican Republic would be contracted for the daily management of the factory

For KIT the proposal to become a shareholder was unexpected. The KIT advisors present during the field visit did not have the authority to decide upon it immediately. They had to first consult with KIT management in the Netherlands. The rest of the visit was used for collecting relevant information for writing the business plan and particularly on the capitalization of the factory. Several scenarios were developed, discussed and negotiated but no agreement was reached during the visit.

The request from Tradin and Conacado triggered the KIT management to reconsider its role as advisor in pro-poor business. Becoming a shareholder would give KIT more influence on the decision making in a company. The opportunity gave a strong impulse to the idea of setting up the Annona sustainable investment fund, together with SPF and ABN AMRO (see case 5, box 2.9).

Meantime, back in the Netherlands, the business plan was written and presented to the SPF. In this business plan a different division of shares was proposed. KIT opted for a larger share in the company, namely 30%. Tradin and Conacado would each hold 35%. Finally, in March 2007, SPF approved the business plan, but only under very strict conditions in order to minimize risks. But one month later ABN-AMRO withdrew from the plan.

There were some other difficulties, both with regard to the local partners as with other financers involved. In the Dominican Republic the relationship between the managing director of Conacado and Tradin worsened and there appeared to be no trust. In the Netherlands the remaining financing party, SPF, resigned. There was also confusion about the delivery of an investment plan. It was also not clear why Conacado remained silent in this confusing period. Had it become scared of its competition (see box 2.5) or did the incentives to become involved in cocoa processing disappear because of the enormous price increases for raw (conventional) cocoa, (which lowered the added value/profit margin of processed cocoa)?

Although, in September 2007, KIT found other interested funders, namely Rabobank International and the Rabobank Foundation, Tradin also lost interest. Now the momentum was gone and all actors gave up on the initiative, including KIT. One year later, in August 2008, Tradin was building its own processing factory in the USA and Conacado was renting the cocoa factory in the Dominican Republic to test its suitability.

> **Box 2.5. Cocoa export oligopoly in the Dominican Republic**
>
> *"Cocoa, money, women: the more the better"*
>
> Historically in the Dominican Republic there have been four dominant exporters accounting for 90-95 percent of total cocoa exports. The two largest firms (Rizek and Roig) accounted for about 70-75 percent of all exports. In the past fifteen years, this domination has been challenged by Conacado. In 2002 the coop represented 25% of all cocoa farmers and had the highest market share of all exporters. The members of Conacado have their own cocoa plantations and use Conacado as a vehicle to market their own produce. Conacado particularly dominates the market for Hispaniola and certified organic cocoa, but recently Rizek also entered this market. Other producer groups established in the 1990s, most notably Aprocaci and Yacao, are also experiencing growth in market share, focusing on Hispaniola and organic cocoa.
>
> The small number of exporters makes for an oligopoly market structure in which prices vary little. On the one hand the 'big four' of exporters, including Conacado's president, meet once a month to have a cup of coffee and to fix prices. But on the other hand, due to the competitive market in which the exporters operate, they do not hesitate to use violence and threats especially towards 'the new kid' Conacado and their staff.

KIT Reflections on changing roles

In the initial partnership, Tradin and Conacado were the joint venture partners. KIT was advisor and mediator, SPF provided capital and the ABN-AMRO Bank would deliver financial expertise.

Then KIT was asked to step in as financer investor, in order to balance the commercial interests and at the same time ensure a Dutch majority in the venture. KIT would initially have a 4% stake in the business. From facilitator KIT became a (modest) business partner and shareholder but still without much influence in decision making.

An important lesson for KIT was that decision-making power and influence on the mission of a sustainable enterprise only comes when you are a business partner with a significant equity share. Acquiring decision-making power in business ventures is important because only then you can assure the inclusion of smallholders and sustainability principles of the business. As a result of this realization, the idea to start a sustainable investment fund with SPF and ABN-AMRO was born. By means of capital from the fund, KIT could have a larger share in the business. The other partners agreed upon this because they would have to put in less equity in the joint venture. KIT thus would become a major shareholder with would help to safeguard the pro-poor aspects of the business.

Pro-poor business vs. conventional business approaches

It is crucial to be clear and honest about each partner's mission of joining a sustainable venture. There are some differences between a pro-poor business approach and a more conventional business approach. Private-sector for-profit businesses tend to rush the planning and start-up process because 'time is money'. It is important to be prepared to counter such pressure and to emphasise the development-side of the process, particularly when values other than making profit are aimed for. In this case, KIT was mainly interested in developing a good business opportunity for cocoa farmers, including local investment in the supply chain, providing access to affordable credit, and capacity building.

In addition, direct communication with and clear involvement from the local business partner (the cooperative) and its members is crucial for a pro-poor business. A lack of understanding and mistrust in each other's motivations to join a new venture must be prevented through a Memorandum of Understanding that clearly indicates the mission and vision of the business, as well as each partner's roles and responsibilities. This key document can help assure commitments, stimulate transparency and avoid surprises of unspoken interests or hidden cards in a later stage of the game. Documenting meetings and any verbal agreements are equally important to prevent misunderstandings.

Internal measures need to be taken when moving from an advisor's role to a finance-investor with shares. Advisors do not automatically have the mandate to set up business operations just because, all of a sudden, money is at stake and risks need to be taken. Doing business also requires a degree of internal reorganization, new skills and the development of new systems and structures.

Unfortunately the joint venture failed. This might have been prevented by more thoroughly screening the business partners on their motivation and true expectations of setting up a business.

Case 4. Processing biodiesel from jatropha with smallholders in Mali

By Bart de Steenhuijsen-Piters and Hugo Verkuijl

Overview

Mali Biocarburant SA is a considered response to the worldwide trend to convert biomass into liquid fuels. Compared to fossil fuels, biofuels are better for the environment, but only if they are produced in a sustainable way. This initiative is about generating biofuels from plants that are harvested from land stretching along the roadside – or by integrating jatropha into existing farming systems, improving crop yields. Jatropha is resistant to drought and grows on poorer soils where other crops fail. It is therefore ideally suited to protecting cultivated fields from wind and rain erosion.

The aim of this business initiative is to establish an enterprise that produces biofuel in a way that supplements farmers' incomes and contributes to poverty alleviation. Geared towards smallholder farmers in Mali, it is an initiative that can be integrated into existing agricultural activities while optimizing positive environmental impact. Jatropha diesel has a combustion efficiency of 23%, only slightly below fossil diesel with 24%.

Farmers harvest jatropha pods from hedgerows surrounding their crop fields and sell the seeds to a local farmers' union. The farmers union adds value to the product by extracting jatropha oil. Returning the press cake to farmers' fields improves soil fertility and soil structure, and the jatropha oil is sold to Mali Biocarburant SA. Mali Biocarburant SA refines the jatropha oil into biodiesel that is sold on the local market. Another by-product of the refining process is glycerin which is sold to a local women's group that produces soap.

The joint venture is a company set up in 2007 by KIT and financed through public and private investments. The farmers' union is a shareholder in the joint venture, providing services to farmers and ensuring that the local population benefits from the initiative.

How a biofuel business was born

During the 1970s and 1980s, KIT and local partners encouraged Malian farmers to plant jatropha in the hedgerows of their fields in order to protect them against erosion. Jatropha's potential for producing high quality oil that could be used for biofuel was investigated in the 1990s.

Jatropha goes global

In 2004, KIT began promoting the idea of producing biodiesel in Mali from jatropha oil. Today, Mali has more than 20,000 kilometres of jatropha hedges. In a Newsweek article of February 19, 2007 Jatropha was referred to as "the Cinderella of the plant world: throw a seed in the poorest soil on the planet, and up comes a bush that will likely last 50 years." According to Newsweek[4], Norwegian, Indian and British companies are racing to buy up or lease enormous swaths of African land for jatropha plantations. UK-based D1 Oils has bought 20,000 hectares in Malawi and 15,000 hectares in Zambia. India's IKF Tech has requested government leases for a combined total of 150,000 hectares in Swaziland, Mozambique and South Africa. Worldwide Bio Refineries, a U.K. firm, has 40,000 hectares set aside for production in Nigeria, with planting beginning in May 2009. Countries such as Mali and Mozambique have initiated special task forces for the promotion of jatropha. How will the creation of large-scale plantations of jatropha affect smallholders and livestock keepers in Sub-Saharan Africa? How 'green' are these biodiesel production systems? How can jatropha production be more closely integrated into the existing farming systems to achieve large-scale adoption and benefits through the involvement of hundreds of thousands of smallholders?

In 2005, KIT conducted a feasibility study in Mali that showed that if the cost of diesel stayed at current levels, locally-produced biodiesel could be priced competitively and sold on the local market. At this stage KIT saw an opportunity to develop a commercially viable business activity, but that assuring positive impacts on smallholder farmers' livelihoods would not be automatic. Merging the commercial and development goals required both a pro-poor business plan, as well as an experienced agency that could implement the plan. KIT decided to engage itself and become a key actor in the business development process.

A search for suitable partners for a joint venture took place in 2006, and a pro-poor business plan was jointly developed by KIT, SPF, PPP and Malian partners Interagro and the Union Locale des Sociétés Coopératives des Producteurs de Pourghère (ULSPP). This plan stipulated how the enterprise should be developed and made into a profitable business. It also explains how smallholders benefit by planting jatropha in their farms, from selling the pods to the farmers' union and spells out representation of this union as a shareholder and board member. In this way, development goals joined the commercial goals in business planning. Mali Biocarburant SA was established under Malian law immediately upon approval by investors.

KIT has 40% of shares and provides the CEO, and chairman of the board from its own staff, who work together on implementing the business plan and monitoring the dual goals. These are clearly formulated and included in the articles of establishment of Mali Biocarburant SA. Accordingly, the performance of the company is evaluated in terms of commercial success, and on the basis of social and environmental impacts.

Currently in the pilot phase, Mali Biocarburant has an operating budget of €820.000. The Netherlands Government awarded a start-up subsidy of €490.000 through its Programme for Co-operation with Emerging Markets (PSOM) which encourages Dutch investments in

---

[4] Newsweek From the magazine issue dated Feb 19, 2007 The Cinderella Plant. Africans Used To Think Jatropha Was A Worthless Bush. Now It May Be An Important New Source Of Energy. By Karen Palmer | http://www.newsweek.com/id/68387. Access date 23 November 2009.

emerging markets. The other five investors contributed €330.000 in private equity, which is reflected in the company's shareholder structure. Mali Biocarburant SA was formally registered as a company in Mali in 2007. An innovative business arrangement is the inclusion of the farmers' union ULSPP as partner, shareholder and member of the Board of Directors. Investing in a start-up company in Mali is also a new departure for the Dutch Railway Pension Fund SPF, another shareholder in the joint venture. Box 2.6 presents the business actors involved. Box 2.7 illustrates how this pro-poor business will benefit local farmers.

Box 2.6. Business actors

KIT Holding B.V. was setup in 2006. KIT Holding B.V. is an active shareholder in the partnership.

ULSPP, a farmers' union with local commitment, networks and representing farmers' interests.

SPF, a foreign investor with capital, financial knowledge and risk management knowledge.

Interagro, which purchases the biodiesel and distributes it, with its local knowledge and networks.

PSOM, a public investment program through the Netherlands Ministry of Economic Affairs, provided 60% of total investments.

Power Pack Plus, a company with technical knowledge and knowledge of African business practice.

One of KIT's objectives is to learn from, and share its experience with private enterprise development that reduces poverty. By making this a successful pro-poor, environmentally friendly and profitable business KIT aspires to become a player in the area of sustainable business. However, KIT does not intend to become a long-term player in the biodiesel industry. KIT will maintain its position in MBSA for the duration of the PSOM project (January 2007 – January 2010).

KIT's exit strategy includes the following parameters:
- Three audited annual reports of MBSA (2007-2009) showing that the business is profitable. These reports should also show that the business includes a farmer organization as a shareholder (dividends paid and shareholder value) and the contribution of the business to farmers' income through the sale of jatropha nuts.
- KIT will offer its shares to the other business partners and/or possibly a third party. This third party should clearly respect the mission of MBSA.
- KIT has documented its participation in MBSA.

> **Box 2.7. How local farmers are expected to benefit**
>
> - New jobs for about 120 people and spin-off benefits for 80,000 families.
> - Additional income for smallholders, estimated at 1250 FCFA/day (Euro 1.90/day).
> - A strengthened producer organization and strengthened local capacity for entrepreneurship, management and governance.
> - Reduced soil erosion due to hedges of jatropha.
> - A secure, clean source of about 1,000,000 litres of biodiesel per month is expected to be produced by Mali Biocarburant within six years.
> - Sale and use of organic fertilizer from the press cake (32,000 kg/week), a production by-product.
> - Enhanced influence and autonomy of farmers through their union, with a decision-making role within the company.
> - Profit for the farmers' union in the form of company dividends.

Overcoming constraints

During the start-up phase of the enterprise various constraints were encountered and the CEO faced numerous challenges implementing the business plan.

Business initiatives with multiple stakeholders, such as Mali Biocarburant SA, are more time consuming and therefore potentially less competitive than single stakeholder initiatives. It takes a long time to find good partners, to carry out due diligence and to reach consensus on how to set up the venture. Insufficient time was given to build these partnerships, which caused partnership attrition during the first phase of the venture. Initial partners were replaced by more committed ones. For example, a Malian investor identified during the business plan development proved unable to raise the capital required and was replaced.

The farmers' organization and its members were not used to the role of shareholder in a private company. Considerable time and effort was needed to inform them of all the advantages and risks. Moreover, shareholding requires levels of organization – including internal transparency and good governance – that need to be in place prior to obtaining shares. Many farmers' organizations do not qualify for bank loans to buy shares. Shareholding needed capacity building and a degree of reorganization for the farmers' organization to become eligible. Members of farmers' organizations must fully understand what is happening and how they can benefit from shareholding. Creating this awareness is not an easy task for a farmers' organization with thousands of members.

A common code for the Jatropha bio fuel sector is lacking and therefore there are no clear guidelines to set up sustainable Jatropha biodiesel businesses. Mali Biocarburant SA is working with small-scale farmers, but competitors are planning to set up jatropha plantations, using large subsidies. This may undermine or reduce the competitiveness of the venture and have negative side effects. Looking at the long-term scenario, after KIT exits the venture, without a common agreed code there is no assurance that the venture will continue to pursue pro-poor sustainable principles as KIT does. This may harm the position of the poor as well as the environment.

After the successful pilot phase MBSA is now developing a national and regional up-scaling strategy. More than 5000 farmers have planted jatropha as intercrop in their fields, plants are growing well, the enterprise is fully operational and will produce biodiesel from jatropha nuts as from this year. By 2010 the first jatropha plants will be in full maturity, allowing the factory to produce at its full capacity. Lessons from the pilot phase will inform the plans for the expansion of the venture. For example, we will first communicate the economic opportunities to farmers and their organizations, facilitate planting jatropha, assess the farmers' organizations and identify capacity development needs, start a trajectory of organizational strengthening and select reliable local business partners. Well organized farmers, jatropha planting and committed local partners are all preconditions for establishing new biodiesel processing units. If these conditions are met, investments will follow.

KIT's changing role
A wealthy northern institution like KIT can be treated by a business partner as a provider of 'easy money' in the form of public subsidy. When this does not materialize, partners may withdraw from providing the agreed amount of equity capital. In the case of Mali Biocarburant several changes in partners were made during the inception phase. Some partners thought KIT would only be an financer-investor and not an active shareholder.

KIT adhered to its pro-poor business engineer role. Providing the equity capital, required to obtain shares, proved to be the best test of partnership commitment. We have learnt that a business associate cannot be selected only on the basis of verbal commitment to pro-poor business or active involvement in engineering the business plan. The dual goals of developing business and reducing poverty need to be substantiated by evidence that the partner has a commitment to principles of corporate social responsibility. Additionally, particular attention has to be given to the solvability of the partner and references from other businesses the partner is involved in.

Designing for pro-poor impact
The business plan developed by KIT and partners benefited from a long track record of KIT work in Mali, as well as personal networks of the CEO. KIT has worked continuously in Mali since the late sixties resulting in a deep knowledge of the country, its institutions and its people. It proved nevertheless difficult to match the views and attitude of Dutch investors with the reality found on the ground in Mali and the pro-poor ambitions of KIT. More than 10 versions of the business plan had to be developed and presented in The Netherlands, adjusting figures and internal organization to the views of 'hard core' investors who have never been in Mali.

Merging the reality of farmers in rural Mali and the aspirations of Dutch investors was the biggest challenge encountered during the business plan development phase. It is sometimes tempting to listen to the more outspoken of the two worlds, which will however give rise to false expectations and inconsistencies in implementation. A big lesson from this process is that spending ample time and effort on careful design in order to get the highest possible pro-poor impact, is always worthwhile and pays off during the implementation phase. Managing business culture and negotiating stakeholder interests is often given insufficient attention in pro-poor business engineering. The process goes far beyond writing the business plan. DO not be surprised if it takes more than a year to achieve agreement and commitment among stakeholders concerned.

Towards good governance

Farmers' representation and farmers' organizations play a critical role in KIT's pro-poor business design. We believe that a sustainable venture should be well rooted in its environment and that farmers should have a voice in important institutions, such as a successful business venture that gives access to markets. In the case of Mali Biocarburant SA we choose to involve a federation of jatropha producers as shareholders and board members.

The federation had to be established for this reason and it was foreseen that SNV, a Dutch NGO, would assist and strengthen the capacities of this federation. The idea of including the federation in the governance of the business venture was well received in Mali by farmers and politicians. The approach was taken as a genuine desire for doing ethical business and not only pursuing foreign interests. But old habits proved to be harder to change than expected. A local politician quickly dominated the federation and far too little attention was given to membership mobilization and transparency.

When funds from the CO_2 compensation scheme had to be distributed, personal interests overshadowed community goals. The Dutch CEO was pulled into an obscure world of power play and local politics, which could only be neutralized with major pressure from the Board and networks of the CEO.

We conclude that capacity development of the federation did not keep pace with the speed of business development. Strengthening a farmers' organization for active participation in the governance of a business venture is required before this is put into effect. Moreover, a sound policy of transparency and membership communication is needed before benefits can be managed and shared.

Besides clear governance structures a pro-poor business venture in Mali needs leadership and reliable management. Foreign investors expect financial administration that adheres to all the criteria they apply themselves, irrespective of the local conditions. Timely and transparent book keeping is essential for preserving the support of foreign investors. This is important because business implementation is never a straight forward application of the business plan. In practice, many adjustments have to be made in response to unforeseen events or new opportunities encountered. The CEO needs the confidence of the investors to make these adjustments; therefore communication skills are important assets of business leadership.

But the CEO is also responsible for the local integration of the business plan in a social environment that has great expectations. These are not only related to issues of fair price setting and trade relations with farmers. Mali Biocarburant operates in an 'economy of scarcity' characterized by great community needs and personal relations that act as safety nets. Once successful, the managers feel pressure at all levels to help out in case of personal needs.

In the case of Mali Biocarburant a combined leadership of a Dutch CEO and a Malian deputy has so far been effective in dealing with such constraints to sustainable business development. A balance has been found between business goals and community support, for which a combined leadership provides the best basis.

Case 5. Yiriwa SA: Setting up a trade house for organic products made in Mali

By Bart de Steenhuijsen-Piters and Kees-Jan van Til

Introduction

This case describes KIT's experiences as catalyst and shareholder of a new trading company in Mali, West Africa. The story begins with AK-O/Mavideniz, which is a company specializing in organizing and coordinating value chains for organic products. In 2007 it approached Agri-ProFocus (APF) with a request to help it establish organic cotton production in West Africa. KIT, ICCO and SNV are members of APF and joined hands with AKO to establish a new trade house in Mali for organic cotton and other rotation crops. Yiriwa SA was founded as a pilot initiative in 2008. That year, it engaged 640 organic cotton farmers and 1055 organic soya and sesame growers. Yiriwa SA has the objective of providing over 30.000 producers by 2012 with assured markets for organic products. Its business strategy is to establish a profitable company that adds local value to agricultural production and that is shared by key actors in the value chains, including farmers' organizations.

Growing organic – responding to demand

Mali is the second largest cotton producer in Sub-Saharan Africa after Burkina Faso. More than 25% of the Mali population depends on cotton for its livelihood. The cotton industry in Mali is in a crisis since 2006 because of decreasing international prices, due to subsidization of farmers in the EU, China and US and a poor organisation of the national market in West Africa. This situation has worsened in 2008 when the Mali government eliminated subsidies to cotton growers, such as the inputs (fertilizer and pesticides) required for production. Consequently many farmers faced decreasing yields per hectare or stopped planting cotton and are turning to other crops, such as groundnuts and maize. Markets for these crops are erratic and impose great risks to rural households. Through the privatisation of Compagnie Malienne pour le Développement des Textiles (CMDT) the Mali Government is effectively withdrawing from the cotton sector altogether.

Organically grown cotton can provide an interesting alternative for farmers. Conventional cotton is the single biggest user of pesticides in agriculture in the world. Organic cotton can be produced in an environmentally friendly way without the use of expensive inputs. The yield of conventional cotton per hectare is higher than that of organic cotton, but the overall income on organic cotton to farmers is higher because cost for inputs are lower and the market offers a price premium compared to conventional cotton. Organic cotton production generates fewer health risks to farmers. Demand for organic cotton is increasing, mainly because of the growing popularity of corporate social responsibility programs of large commercial clothing producers, such as Wal-Mart, Nike and others. Consumers increasingly demand clothing labelled as organic cotton.

Farmers in Mali practice a rotation system with fallow periods. Land under 5-year fallow is generally unpolluted by previous pesticide use. This land can be cultivated for certified organic production. The combination of a growing market for organic cotton with higher, stable prices, a strong market for rotation crops and the availability of fallow land for certified cultivation created an excellent business opportunity and the potential for poverty alleviation and social development. Annona Sustainable Investment Fund/KIT, ICCO and AK-O/Mavideniz, with support from SNV and AgriProFocus, anticipated this opportunity and have been involved in the "Projet Bio-Equitable" since 2007. By 2008 the project evolved into a trade house registered under the name Yiriwa SA. The mission of Yiriwa SA is to reduce rural poverty and enhance rural livelihoods in Mali through development of sustainable trade in organic and fair trade products (box 2.8).

> **Box 2.8. The trade house concept: Yiriwa SA**
>
> In a world of growing complexity and international flows of capital, goods, services and information, new modalities are needed to facilitate and govern these flows. This particularly applies to value chains in developing countries with end consumers in western countries. Such value chains require effective organization with well-linked components and transparent decision making. A characteristic of international value chains is the confrontations of different corporate cultures, and interests that often remain implicit, but frequently causes the early abortion or collapse of newly established value chains.
>
> The conventional cotton-based value chains in Mali were organized through parastatal institutions that conducted almost all chain functions, from input supply, transport and collection to ginning and marketing. The only role for farmers is to grow and harvest the cotton.
> In the case of organic/fair trade production, very few organizations are available at national level to produce, collect, process and sell these products. Due to the absence of such organizations there is little support or incentive for farmers to convert to organic/fair trade production.
>
> The establishment of a trade house in organic/fair trade products in Mali will create new value chains. Trade houses link actors and organize value chains by creating structures, stability and confidence among the actors. Above all, trade houses are mechanisms to enhance chain transparency and provide a forum for merging interests as well as resolving conflicts.

In March 2008 Yiriwa SA was created with the mission to develop sustainable trade in organic and fair trade products and thus reduce rural poverty and enhance rural livelihoods in Mali. With the introduction of organic and fair trade modes of production, people's health and biodiversity will be improved. The roles of Yiriwa SA as a trade house are:

- Organizing organic and fair trade value chains.
- Assisting farmers with technical knowledge for certified production that respects all procurement standards.
- Securing international markets for organically grown produces in Africa such as cotton, sesame and soy over a long period of time.

- Obtaining large volumes of organically grown produces through smallholder production thus generating long term revenues.
- Securing interesting remuneration for the farmers through the payment of organic and fair trade premium prices to farmers.
- Adding local value through processing (ginning, cleaning, grading etc).

KIT reflections

In 2007 AK-O/Mavideniz took the initiative to explore commercial organic production possibilities in West Africa. Because AK-O/Mavideniz knew from experience that the start-up phase for a new business is very costly and difficult, they involved other partners from whom they expected financial support and technical assistance. Process facilitation by AgriProFocus resulted in the involvement of the three partners SNV, Annona/KIT and ICCO. These partners formed a consortium and started working on a business concept that ensured sustainable, pro-poor commerce based on the fair trade principles.

The three investing partners had different reasons to join the venture. AK-O/Mavideniz joined because of commercial interests; ICCO because the venture fit perfectly with their pro-poor cotton interventions in West Africa; and Annona/KIT joined because it allowed them to test their new entrepreneurial business concept in developing countries. SNV participated because of their broad experience with cotton in West Africa. The decision by AgriProFocus to participate was based on its mission to help foster effective collaboration between members (box 2.9).

The local producer organizations were screened during the first missions in Mali and Burkina based on the local experiences of SNV and ICCO. The selected producer organizations were already partners of SNV.

Box 2.9. Who is behind Yiriwa S.A.

AK-O/Mavideniz specializes in large scale production, sales and marketing of organic cotton. AK-O/Mavideniz is one of the shareholders and a board member of Yiriwa SA. AK-O/Mavideniz handles marketing for all Yiriwa products and is the major commercial partner in the venture.

KIT is an investor (through the Annona Fund - see below), and also directly supports Yiriwa SA and its farmers' capacity development programme. KIT provided the manager of Yiriwa SA until its formal registration and delivered specific technical knowledge on organic production. KIT is chairman of Yiriwa SA's Board of Directors. KIT monitors and evaluates the performance of Yiriwa SA based on sustainable business opportunities and poverty impacts.

Interchurch Organization for Development C-operation (ICCO) supports of cotton producers in West Africa. In Mali and Burkina Faso ICCO collaborates with the Swiss organization Helvetas on organic cotton production. With more than five years experience in the organic cotton business, ICCO brings broad knowledge and a network of contacts to Yiriwa SA and facilitates links with the West African cotton sector. ICCO owns 24% of capital investments and shares and finance the Capacity Development Plan that is being executed by the SNV. They are member of the board of Yiriwa SA.

The Netherlands Development Organization (SNV) has much experience in supporting Malian producer organizations. Project sites in Mali and Burkina Faso were selected based on the presence of SNV. They work closely with the farmers' organizations and have a large network within the organic cotton sector in both countries. SNV manages a Capacity Development Plan to strengthen the farmers' organizations participating in Yiriwa SA.

Farmers' organizations play an important role as the key agencies in improving livelihoods in rural areas. Especially primary village cooperatives have the confidence of their members, represent large segments of rural society, deliver services and represent farmers' interests at different levels. They are trained through the Capacity Development Plan to support the organic/fair-trade production and deliver high quality products to Yiriwa SA.

Agri-ProFocus (APF) is a Dutch consortium of 26 donor agencies, credit institutions, fair trade organizations, training institutes and knowledge institutions. APF's objective is to promote strong rural producer organizations that can play a crucial role in economic development, strengthen democracy and alleviate poverty in rural areas. They promote ties between their members and the business sector to help producer organizations fulfill this important role. APF responded to AK-O/Mavideniz's initial request for assistance and facilitated the initiative in its early stages.

Annona Sustainable Investment Fund was established in December 2008 and is owned by Holding KIT BV, the Railways Pension Fund (SPF) and the Pension Fund Public Transportation (SPOV). The idea to set up a sustainable investment fund came from KIT, which is a knowledge institute in international cooperation and development. The idea was set off by the notion that through enterprising the leverage on poverty impact would become higher. The fund is based on Corporate Social Responsibility policies.

The purpose of the fund is creating revenues by means of investing, managing and selling shares in starting and already existing enterprises in agriculture, agri-business, biomedical activities, sustainable energy, para medical activities and eco tourism in Latin America and Africa. The fund has two tasks which are realizing a final average financial ROI of 11% and promoting the development of the private sector in a way that helps to tackle poverty. It aims to do this through setting up 10 to 15 sustainable agri businesses.

From the start there were many issues of trust and confidence among the partners. Some natural distrust is to be expected between commercial organizations and socially oriented development organizations. The latter is said to be too soft, too participative and too less action-oriented, while the first is often considered too profit oriented without considering the social needs and cultural context. These are classical conflicts, which also occurred in this case. During the first year of the collaboration a lot of time was taken up in meetings, fine tuning the business plan, checking the positions and ideas of others and determining the individual interests of every participant. During this decision making process the parties gradually started to know each other, which created confidence and trust. This finally resulted in a Memorandum of Understanding (MoU) between the partners, stating the roles and responsibilities of each other.

The second trust issue was between the local organizations in Mali and Burkina Faso on the one hand and Yiriwa SA on the other hand. Yiriwa SA was viewed as a commercial organization that was going to make a lot of money selling African products to northern/European markets.

This image was created during the first visits of AK-O/Mavideniz in Mali and Burkina Faso. AK-O/Mavideniz is one on the biggest players in organic cotton production in the world, and showed production estimations in Mali and Burkina of 30.000 tons of cotton where Helvetas has been unable to produce more than 800 tons after seven years of intervention in the field. Dutch actors wanted to speed-up the process, while in Mali and Burkina Faso organizations needed more time to familiarize with the initiative. This scared off some organizations among which Helvetas and the National Union of Cotton Producers in Burkina Faso. Burkina Faso decided not to participate in Yiriwa because they were afraid to lose control over the organic market in their country. Helvetas also greatly increased their production goals (also to 30,000 tons!) and refused in a friendly way to collaborate.

The government-owned ginner, CMDT in Mali, afraid to lose control over their cotton suppliers, was very reluctant to allow Yiriwa SA access to their production zones. Overcoming this deadlock needed direct intervention to educate the farmers' organizations. SNV informed and mobilized the farmers, emphasizing from the start the ecological, environmental and sustainable side of Yiriwa SA. This awareness-raising approach succeeded in convincing the farmers.

Special efforts organized by ICCO, KIT and AK-O/Mavideniz were necessary in Mali and Burkina Faso to explain the purpose of Yiriwa SA to producer organizations and obtain their cooperation. This only succeeded in Mali, where Yiriwa SA was registered early 2008.

To test the grounds and manage financial risks it was decided to start with an inception phase. This phase started on March 5, 2008 and ended on January 31st 2009. Outputs to be achieved were defined in the MoU signed between all parties (see figure 2.1).

Figure 2.1. Agreed milestones during first year.

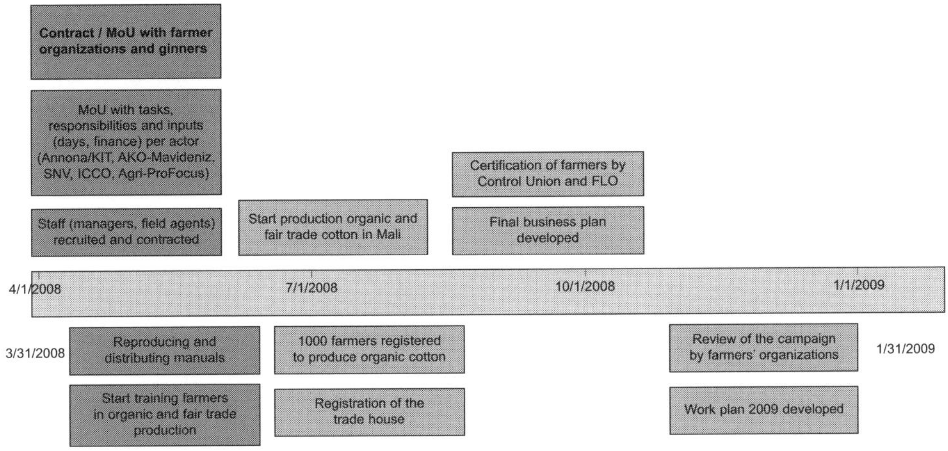

The dates of these outputs had to be changed several times. This was partly due to the unpredictable nature of the work in the field and overly optimistic production estimations. In early phases of this initiative it was very difficult to match interests and expectations of all parties involved. This resulted in unrealistic targets, some of which were made to satisfy the perceived needs of early investors.

Shareholders of Yiriwa SA decided that a critical review of the inception phase and its deliverables was required to decide whether to continue or conclude the initiative. By mid-2008 it became clear that targets set would not be achieved. The number of registered organic cotton growers remained below expectation, but there were more farmers than expected producing organic soya and sesame. The buyer for the organic cotton – to be identified by AK-O – remained unknown to the consortium for too long.

Partners started to question the positive market assessment and prognosis for the future, as the global financial crisis started to have its effects on organic cotton trade. Internationally, prices for organic cotton dropped due to large stocks and reduced demand. This put strong pressure on AK-O/Mavideniz to reconsider its general procurement and investment policy. Due to these unforeseen events, AK-O could not provide shareholder capital as agreed. On top of that it took time to find a buyer with the desired profile.

During the second half of 2008 the delays and marketing problems put significant stress on the partnership. Were we wrong in our enthusiasm about the prospects for organic cotton? Could the company honor its obligations to the farmers who took the risk to plant cotton? And what about the future, was the market sufficiently stable to support the growth of Yiriwa SA and, indirectly for 30,000 Malian farmer households?

Partners met many times and tensions emerged, but were discussed and eased. At the end of 2008, confidence was restored when AK-O/Mavideniz proposed a client for the organic cotton. Yiriwa SA paid farmers the prices promised at the beginning of the campaign, reducing losses of the pilot phase to a minimum. A new business plan was drafted and discussed among all partners. Farmers and their organizations were very positive about the campaign, including the role of Yiriwa SA and its technical staff.

Although the target number of farmers was not met in 2008, now many farmers started to register for the new campaign. The business plan was no longer restrained by the number of farmers interested, but by Yiriwa's capacity to secure technical support to farmers and assure quality produce to its international clients. As such, the business plan and its growth scenario was developed in view of Yiriwa's organizational capacities (table 2.2).

Table 2.2. Production, farmers and technical staff estimates (source: business plan 2009)

Estimation	2008/2009	2009/2010	2010/2011	2011/2012	2012/2013	2013/2014
Bio cotton tons	79	500	2,000	4,500	10,000	17,500
Bio sesame tons	400	1,000	1,500	1,750	2,000	2,500
Bio soya tons	42	500	1,000	1,500	2,000	2,500
Bio groundnuts tons	0	1,500	3,000	5,000	7,000	9,000
Total number of farmers	1,732	6,000	17,000	21,000	30,000	36,000
Total technical staff	9	15	40	45	60	71

In order to pay farmers a fair price and a premium for their organic cotton, it became necessary to include ginning in Yiriwa's business activities. Outsourcing ginning to the CMDT was too expensive, reducing profits and thus payment of fair prices to farmers. In addition to the core business plan, an additional business plan for investments in a ginning factory was made. By early 2009 shareholders agreed on Yiriwa's future and transferred their share capital for continued investment (table 2.3 illustrates the composition of shareholders). A parallel Capacity Development Programme was further developed to support producer organizations and agreed for technical and financial support by ICCO, SNV and Annona/KIT by mid 2009.

Table 2.3. Shareholder composition

Shareholder	Shares %
Annona	28
ICCO	24
AK-O/Mavideniz	24
Farmers (through the farmer's association)	24
Total investment in Euros	1,600,000

KIT's changing role: from advisor to active shareholder

In the early stage of the initiative AgriProFocus approached KIT, known for its knowledge on cotton production in West Africa, to facilitate a partnership between AK-O/Mavideniz, several NGOs and farmers in Mali and Burkina Faso. The process of partnership development proved to be harder than expected. Parties were not used to each other's corporate behavior, expectations were quite different and each party had considerable assumptions about the other parties. Moreover, it proved difficult to merge the process taking place in the offices in the Netherlands and day to day reality in West Africa. AK-O/Mavideniz had no substantial experience with doing business in West Africa and expected farmers and their organizations to respond quickly and positively to the opportunity offered. Moreover, AK-O/Mavideniz believed that SNV could represent the farmers, and that deals could be agreed with SNV. But SNV cannot act on behalf of farmers and is only in a position that they can provide advice and technical support to their organizations.

Meanwhile, ICCO and KIT had agreed on a deal with AK-O/Mavideniz, who was eager to do business but was also concerned about the [momentum on] stability of the global market for organic cotton and felt that action was required. The CEO of AK-O/Mavideniz felt misunderstood because KIT or ICCO do not have full knowledge of the reality of cotton business and complex trade operations. AK-O/Mavideniz expected also that the NGOs would be willing to finance all investments in developing the organic cotton value chain. They would bring in their knowledge and goodwill as inputs, which had to be valued by the other actors as serious assets. But no NGO was willing to pre-finance such investments without the necessary trust and documentation. NGOs need programme documents and work plans in order to convince internal decision makers of the necessity to raise finance. Clear references to targets, outputs, outcomes and impacts are required, such as how much poverty will be alleviated with a given investment. This was a world completely unknown to AK-O/Mavideniz.

A comprehensive business plan was required in which investors had to be identified to finance the organic cotton business. Among the partners, only KIT had the necessary experience and know-how to develop such a business plan. KIT was asked to write the business plan for which ICCO provided partial financing. The process of writing the business plan was difficult and it took time to obtain the agreement of all parties, including new investors. Some actors such as

SNV were not used to the rather 'hard business manner' now deployed by KIT. But the business plan had to be eligible for private equity investors, who have their dominant modes of assessment, which have to be respected. In this process, KIT was bridging two extreme worlds of corporate investors in the Netherlands – having no experience with investing in African business – and smallholder farmers in West Africa struggling to survive – being disappointed in the cotton industry.

To keep moving and improve communications KIT contracted an ex-SNV staff as manager of the project. He contracted a deputy manager from Mali and together they became the face and voice of the pilot initiative. Now farmers and their organizations gained trust in the project, while Dutch investors also became acquainted with the manager behind the plans. The pilot phase was successful in building trust and confidence. When the business plan was finally ready in early 2009, ICCO and the Annona Sustainable Investment Fund approved the investments and transferred the capital required to expand the business.

KIT started out as an advisor and mediator in this initiative, gradually became the business developer and ended as an active shareholder of Yiriwa SA through its shares in the Annona Fund established by KIT. KIT continues to provide knowledge and advice to the capacity strengthening programme that is being managed by SNV and ICCO. Playing these various roles has allowed KIT to respond to evolving needs by the parties involved. KIT has been able to take on a variety of roles that create a high degree of flexibility. However, for the partners this was confusing and it was not always clear why KIT was engaged in the process and what its primary interests were. KIT affirmed that its core business is poverty alleviation, and that it can contribute to this goal in different ways.

An essential lesson learnt from this process was that more attention should be paid to an early assessment of interests of all actors and their assumptions about other parties. Bridging the world of commercial actors and investors in Europe and smallholder farmers in Africa is a very complicated process that cannot be rushed. The process is defined by critical steps that have to be followed in order to build trust and confidence. All actors must understand this process from the very beginning and adjust their expectations and planning accordingly.

Seeking pro-poor impact

This business case offers alternatives for cotton producers that are experiencing severe economic problems. It offers employment and income improvements for small-scale farmers and will enable them to work in a more environmental and sustainable way. The specific element in this business case is the commercial opportunities the trade house offers for the farmers in terms of participation in the investments (shareholder), decision-making and profit sharing. They are not only considered as producers of agricultural products, but also as members in the board of the trade house, what will lead to more ownership and awareness of all aspects in the market chain. The parallel capacity development program will help farmers not only to produce organic cotton according to standards and regulations, but also to get organized and engage in decision making processes of Yiriwa SA, such as during the annual shareholder meeting. KIT has actively advocated for the more integral involvement of farmers. During the development of the business plan all options for active corporate social responsibility were explored. The goal of doing sustainable business was included in the statutes of Yiriwa SA and requires the board to monitor not only financial performance but also impact on society and environment.

Governance

This case illustrates that a clear business structure such as Yiriwa SA – involving important actors as shareholders - has helped to create a transparent organizational structure in which roles and responsibilities are well defined. When relations between actors are not clear, speculations may persist and disturb the process of trust building. However, the process towards clear relations in terms of who is shareholder, who is service provider, how are shares divided and who has a seat on the board is very difficult when actors are diverse in terms of corporate and cultural background. Interests have to surface in order to negotiate shares. This process cannot be hastened, but should be handled with care. For KIT it is important to communicate from the beginning what its mission and intentions are. Changing roles over time may be necessary, but should be well understood by other actors.

One of the lessons learnt is that – in the end – all actors remaining in the initiative play their rather natural role and are appreciated for that. AK-O/Mavideniz has identified the end-buyer and keeps on coordinating the value chain. ICCO is shareholder in Yiriwa SA and advocates as such for farmers' interests. It also finances the capacity strengthening programme and supervises its implementation by SNV. SNV focuses on this programme and continues supporting farmers' organizations. These are building up their levels of organization and efficiency and will become more and more important as shareholders of Yiriwa and service providers to farmers, such taking over roles of ICCO, SNV and KIT.

Finally, KIT keeps supporting Yiriwa SA and the capacity strengthening programme with knowledge. In the role as board chairman, guidance is given to good governance and managing the interests of all parties involved. Annona will exit after seven years and sell its shares, preferably to farmers' organizations or local investors. And the farmers? If Yiriwa SA sustains itself and expands its markets, then more and more farmers will benefit from a regular source of income. Their production will be increasingly environmentally friendly, reducing health risks or all people working on these fields. Processing operations will create employment and add local value.

We hope to see a cotton industry emerging in Mali that continues producing fabrics without the need for costly inputs that damage the health of farmers and the agro-ecosystem.

3 Facilitating pro-poor businesses: what have we learned?

By Marije Boomsma, Anna Laven and Bart de Steenhuijsen-Piters

Lessons from cases

KIT has been involved in pro-poor business development for almost five years. As a facilitator of chain development KIT brings business partners together, provides expertise and ensures that business ventures deliver benefits to all actors in the chain. From this position it was logical for KIT to be involved as an advisor in partnerships between different actors. In some cases, however, the advisory role has limitations. As an advisor with no mandate to intervene and no stake in the business as such, it can be difficult to safeguard pro-poor business objectives, which is core to KIT's mission. Without a mandate to intervene it is also challenging to build trust between the local actors, as happened in the ginger case. In such cases we learned that it is more effective to play the mediator role. We furthermore learned that without taking risks, without a stake in the business, our role as mediator was still limited. We needed to be an investor. This would also distinguish us from other organizations involved in pro-poor business development.

From being an advisor, KIT diversified its roles and became a potential financer-investor in an organic cocoa processing company in the Dominican Republic. Here it turned out that the private sector was mainly interested in quick profit and less in the social bottom line of business. The start-up process took too long for the private sector and they moved on.

KIT learned its lessons and then became key initiator and main investor in two other pro-poor businesses, Yiriwa and Mali Biocarburant. In both cases KIT took the lead and managed the design of the business. Partners were screened on their commitment to sustainable business and time was allocated to involve smallholders in setting up the businesses as well as in managing them.

Before we reflect more generally on KIT's role in pro-poor businesses we will briefly summarize the lessons learned from the specific cases.

In the *Unifine ginger case* in Sierra Leone, the main lesson learned was that to be an effective mediator with the authority to intervene, KIT had to obtain the mandate of all stakeholders in a value chain, including the support organizations. This status is not acquired automatically. Effective mediation requires a thorough partner check on vision and, most importantly, time to become trusted by all stakeholders. This conflicts with the aim of companies that are usually in a rush to do business. This conflict is what makes facilitating chain partnerships so challenging.

In addition to time, effective mediation requires local representation. In the Unifine case, KIT was not sufficiently present in Sierra Leone. Partly because of being a foreign entity, KIT was unable to win the trust of the local players and as a result was not given a mandate to act. Another critical lesson is the need to include small producers early in the process. Without their participation the chain will never become pro-poor.

The *tuna case* highlighted our changing role from mediator to advisor. Though all parties agreed that our role as mediator was needed, we were not sufficiently mandated to intervene and enforce implementation of resolutions by all parties. Moreover, we were excluded from internal business processes, such as negotiations on share allocations. It was only after constraints with the capitalization of the business occurred that we could propose fishing associations as shareholders, thus empowering the voice of the poor and enhancing chances that the business would contribute to poverty reduction. As advisor for the fishing associations our role became more transparent to all parties. We were effective in terms of proposing solutions for their involvement and organizational strengthening, but in that role we could not prevent the slowing down of progress in implementing the partnership programme.

KIT entered the *cocoa case* as a financer-investor but soon found that this was not sufficient to achieve its goal of setting up a business with a pro-poor mission. Only by becoming an active shareholder could this mission be safeguarded, because only in this role did KIT have a mandate to act. As with the other cases, partner businesses were impatient and wanted to speed up the process. This hindered setting up the pro-poor function of the business venture and the company was never capitalized. It is key that partners agree on the pro-poor goals of a business at an early stage of the process. Business partners should be carefully selected based on their economic and social ambitions and MoUs must underline these ambitions. Also in this case the local partners, including the farmers, should have been key actors in the preparation phase.

Mali Biocarburant was KIT's first time to engage as an active shareholder. We decided to take shares and provide management and a board member in order to test a new concept based on the dual goal of profitability and pro-poor impacts. We could not identify any other party to whom we could fully trust this experiment. We developed a business plan that would impact on poverty, without compromising the profitability of the business. This required a thorough understanding of opportunities and constraints in their Malian context. We definitely had to get used to this new role and questions about our legitimacy were frequently asked. Did we loose our independence by engaging in a commercial business? Was KIT now seeking profit? We had to explain to the skeptics that we would not abandon our core mission of poverty reduction, but that we were exploring more effective roles for influencing the private sector. Could we have achieved the same impact on poverty if we had stuck to our role as advisor or mediator? It is unlikely that a company such as Mali Biocarburant would have emerged from these modes of facilitation.

In the case of Yiriwa SA we built upon the experience with Mali Biocarburant and decided to assume the role of active shareholder. This role seemed most effective in dealing with the complexity of involving so many parties, the divergence of interests, conflicts in corporate culture and the need for venture capital. The chance that poverty would be impacted was enhanced by the design of the trade house and the formulation of a capacity development plan. Partners were selected on their potential contribution and their complementarity, and this resulted in a complex process of business development full of unexpected events and setbacks. Together with the Dutch NGO ICCO we financed a majority of shares, took seats on the board, and provided a managing director. This created a sound basis for developing a rather difficult business of producing and marketing organically certified products by smallholders. Though the role of active shareholder has been effective to date, we must define and communicate our exit strategy, confirming that our role is temporary and that knowledge as well as shares must at some point be transferred to local parties. Figure 3.1 shows the different roles of the facilitator for each case.

Figure 3.1 Different roles, in different cases

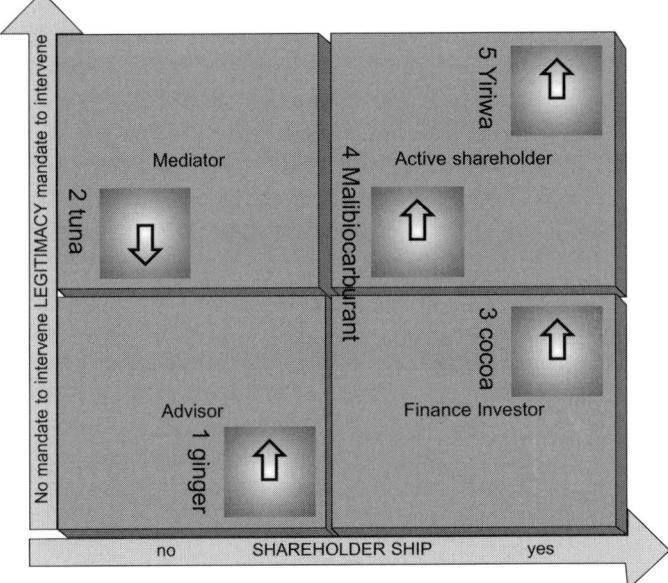

In all cases, the lack of legitimacy frustrated KIT in achieving its pro-poor goals. Without a clear mandate to intervene it proved difficult to ensure that the poor involved in the partnership also actively participate.

Changing positions of pro-poor business partners

Our role in pro-poor business projects has evolved to become more diverse. The pro-poor business sector, involving established businesses that are buying from small producers in developing countries, development organizations and producer groups, is a recent phenomenon. While the private sector could afford to work more independently in the past, a number of developments altered this trend. Market reforms, changes in demand and intensified competition among private firms led to the establishment of more direct relations between established buyers and their suppliers. But such changes have brought their share of problems. Not all the producing countries were ready for this shift, some lacking organization, infrastructure and trust. Also buyers have faced challenges, such as not being fully informed about local business practices and having to invest in strengthening capacity. This situation created demand for additional knowledge, finance and facilitation.

Some large private companies established their own foundations (Royal Dutch Shell, for example), but it has become more common to look for expertise outside their businesses. KIT and other knowledge centres and development organizations have stepped in to take on this role. Having particular knowledge about countries, sectors within countries, cultural practices and established local networks in producing countries, their involvement added value to the private sector. Moreover, development organizations recognized the value of working together with the private sector, to improve their income generating programs for small producers and to make these more sustainable. In attempts by development organizations to stimulate the formation of small private businesses and support their growth, it was common practice to seek advice from other organizations that had specific knowledge in a sector. The advisor was consulted for expertise, without having a stake in the business or project.

The private sector had a different demand for facilitation. They were looking not only for external advice but welcomed a more active and continuous role. They needed mediation between different actors involved in a pro-poor business, actors with different business interests and motives. Besides needing someone to reconcile differences they also needed additional risk capital and participation in governance structures, such as shareholding and boards.

In chapter 1, we presented the relevant issues that must be taken into account when establishing relations with the private sector, namely interest and commitment. In the different cases we have seen that the main motivation for private companies joining partnerships was commercial benefit. A lack of commitment to the pro-poor goals of the partnership was a clear problem in three of the cases: ginger, tuna and cocoa. This is a signal that pro-poor businesses are not yet fully institutionalized. We have seen that other actors outside commercial businesses also face difficulties in participating in this new modality. The roles of different actors in linking business to development cooperation have changed. This makes learning a key aspect of promoting pro-poor business development.

The involvement of a knowledge institute in pro-poor business
Should a knowledge institute, which is originally a not-for-profit organization, take up the role of an investor? Why can't other private actors play this role? Even though we would like the private sector to invest in pro-poor business, from several business examples we have learned that this is not happening. In the ginger, tuna and cocoa cases, the private sector was neither able nor willing to invest in the capacities of smallholders or engage them as partners in business. On top of that there were no capable local organizations to facilitate the process of integrating pro-poor goals in profitable business. Obviously there was a need for an experienced player, such as KIT, with a mission to reduce poverty through private sector development.

It is interesting to see whether we are effective in this new role and whether we, so far, have accomplished our mission. In other words, does the role of engineer-investor lead us to businesses that are visibly pro-poor?

At the time of writing we have invested in two pro-poor business ventures, Mali Biocarburant and Yiriwa SA. Both companies are new and not yet in a mature phase of development. This question can therefore be only partially answered. We can state that in both businesses all partners support the pro-poor nature of the ventures. This means that the bottom line of the company is not just profit making, but that social development and environmental protection are important as well. The exact impact of this strategic direction is not (yet) known. We do know, in the case of Mali Biocarburant, however, that smallholders have more influence in the business through their representation on the board than in other companies. We can also firmly say that farmers are earning additional income because of the business, and that investments are being made in their training and infrastructure. Similar performance results have been logged in the case of Yiriwa SA. Also, organic cotton farmers are being trained, they receive higher prices for the organic cotton than for conventional cotton and they diversify their incomes, which makes them less vulnerable to market and price fluctuations. We have not yet quantified the extent to which these results were caused by KIT's support, nor do we know the wider impact of our interventions.

On the other hand, we do know that KIT took the lead in designing the enterprises. We have clearly influenced their mission statements, including sustainability and pro-poor impacts as targets, the concept of involving smallholders in all stages, and the composition of their governance bodies, such as shareholders and board members. This has been KIT's role.

In the other business cases, in which we were (in the end) only an advisor, we did not have direct influence. In the ginger case and the tuna case, we lost control over the design of the pro-poor enterprises. In the ginger case, we were unable to prevent exclusion of farmers from the business agreements. We did not support local players in developing their capacity. In the tuna case we did not have a mandate to act and therefore could not assure that the business was sufficiently transparent and that conflicting interests were dealt with. In the cocoa case KIT realized too late that the business partners were not committed to pro-poor business goals and that there was no trust among the buyers and suppliers of the organic cocoa.[5]

Contextualizing roles
We conclude from the cases that a facilitation role is optimal only if it is embedded in its context and based on demand. Generally speaking the four roles (advisor, mediator, financer-investor, active shareholder) can co-exist in an organization like KIT, enhancing its degree of freedom to respond to different situations and requests for facilitation. In the past KIT was usually asked to act as advisor or mediator. More recently the new roles of active shareholder and financer-investor were added in response to demand from the private sector. Acting as advisor or mediator, KIT was unsuccessful in influencing the agenda of private parties. Implementation of advice remains voluntary by the private company and cannot be endorsed by the advisor. In contrast, the decision-making power that comes with being a shareholder or even board member strengthens our advocacy for enhancing sustainability. It is not always necessary or even effective, however, for KIT to own shares and engage in management and governance of a firm. We do not want to compete with local parties that are actually important for sustaining a pro-poor business, such as a local venture fund or a bank that is able and willing to provide investment capital. Competing with these local agencies would counteract the autonomous development process. So, can we explore what are effective combinations between facilitation and context/demand?

---

[5] The above hopefully proves the complementarity of shareholding to the other roles of organizations like KIT. We are not advocating against other roles. The roles of advisor and mediator can have positive impact, but only if the circumstances are right.

The effective pro-poor *advisor* works in a context defined by common interests among partners. Trust has been built up over years and the partnership is not challenged by conflicts or incompatible motives. The partners agree on joint goals, but lack specific knowledge or expertise, which is provided by the advisor. Partners welcome the advice and will apply it because it helps them achieve their targets. An advisor can be effective when working for a single client, including a business enterprise, but the advice must either increase the client's knowledge or be in line with corporate policy to be appreciated. Advisors can be contracted to confront a client with, for example, inconsistencies in its corporate policy. Yet, these kinds of assignments remain the domain of top-level advisors with undisputed authority in their field.

The effective *mediator* works in a context of diversity of parties who may have – potentially – conflicting interests. Each of these parties has its own corporate culture and may have prejudiced opinions about the other parties, a situation which we observed in the tuna and Yiriwa cases. They, however, share a common goal that can be achieved only by working together. Mediators are needed to facilitate the process of convergence towards mutual understanding and respect. They must clarify the motives, interests and possible prejudices of each of the parties at an early stage of partnership development. Mediators are effective only when all parties agree to address the problem of divergence when it hinders partnership development, and direct the mediator to intervene. He or she may have to remain involved for an extended period to monitor parties' corporate behavior and implementation of joint agreements.

The *financer-investor* responds to a need for investment and will be effective in terms of pro-poor business when financial gaps are a constraint. The financer-investor not only provides capital for investment, but also offers the knowledge and expertise needed to assess the investment request in its wider economic and social environment. Where other financers decline funding, for example because of perceived risks or inadequate business planning, a financer-investor such as KIT may take up the challenge and mobilize its knowledge to accompany an investment. By thoroughly assessing risks in their context, appropriate responses by the management may be identified and discussed with parties. In the cocoa case, for example, a sound business analysis by KIT revealed that reorganizing the board and management could mitigate risks perceived by conventional investors. Involving farmers' organizations as shareholders could enhance pro-poor impacts. Unfortunately, the business partners rejected these changes.

The *active shareholder* role implies the most engagement of the four facilitation roles. Facilitators become active shareholders as part of the process of pro-poor business development. They use the power vested in shareholders to advocate for the dual role of profitability and pro-poor impact. This role is mainly required in situations defined by various constraints, such as lack of human capacity, potentially conflicting interests between parties, lack of capital or ability to obtain investments and insufficient impact on poverty. The active shareholder provides both capital and knowledge, and may engage in business operations through management. To emphasize the short-term purpose of the role, a clear exit strategy is required, including the transfer of management and governance responsibilities as well as shares.

Assuming management or governance functions will be effective only when combined with human capacity building and transfer of knowledge and expertise to local people. In the case of Mali Biocarburant a new business concept had to be elaborated and tested in order to establish a profitable and pro-poor business. The business plan had to be developed from scratch and KIT had to take financial risks itself to obtain additional investments from other parties. Taking a seat on the board was necessary for ensuring good governance and meeting the requirements imposed by Dutch investors. As an active shareholder, KIT did not compete with local parties because no local business was yet successful in sustainable bio-diesel production. Nor could local venture capital be mobilized to finance the business.

Final reflections
Over the last five years KIT has played different roles in linking private businesses to producer organizations, NGOs and the public sector. Initially KIT's most natural roles were those of advisor and mediator. Over the last two years this has changed and KIT is an active shareholder in pro-poor businesses.

The change – from being a player with little mandate to act to being a full business partner – does not imply that other roles are less important. In cases when no other parties invest in starting a pro-poor business, KIT needs to and wants to play the role of investor and active shareholder for the sake of pro-poor development. Through this new role we have achieved more direct influence on the conditions under which smallholders are active participants in business. The key to these investments is our exit strategy: to step out of these investments after a couple of years when local capacity is in place to run the businesses in a sustainable way. Also key is KIT's continuous focus on learning and sharing experiences in this process. We hope that other organizations like KIT recognize themselves in these roles and are inspired to make similar (or better) choices so that more people will benefit.

Epilogue

"It is easier to make a profitable business more socially responsible, than to turn a socially responsible project into a profitable business."

By Michiel Arnoldus

"What has happened since?"

The activities of KIT described in this book ultimately led to the foundation of the Annona Sustainable Investment Fund, which was officially launched in January 2009. Annona invests in small and medium-sized enterprises in Africa and Latin America by providing equity in combination with loans. It is a separate legal entity from KIT: two Dutch pension funds and KIT are investors in the fund, which has an independent fund manager and an investment committee. KIT acts as an intermediary between entrepreneurs who need funding and the Annona fund. Currently, KIT's main tasks are to evaluate business plans, to coach entrepreneurs in developing a business plan and to develop a local network of partners in Africa and Latin America to increase the stream of promising investment opportunities.

The experiences described in this book led to an important change in KIT's approach to pro-poor business: KIT will no longer write business plans for organizations that want to start a business and then find a manager to execute it. Instead, KIT now looks for an experienced local entrepreneur who already has a plan, and then assists the entrepreneur in improving it. Preferred candidates are entrepreneurs with an existing business that needs upscaling, but start-ups are also welcome if the entrepreneur is willing to invest his/her own money, has relevant experience in both the sector and the country, will commit to the business full-time and will be on site full-time to manage it.

Why local entrepreneurs? Setting up a business in Africa and Latin America is incredibly difficult, and requires a great deal of vision, skill, commitment, cultural understanding and determination. Local entrepreneurs who have invested their personal savings and years of their lives developing an idea into a business are much more likely to have a realistic business model that works, and to go to great lengths to make it work. After all, they have invested everything they own, and it's their own money and future which is at stake. For a manager, on the other hand, it's just a job, while for a Westerner looking to set up or manage a business in the South, it's a great adventure and maybe a long-held dream. But both the manager and Westerner can easily move on to the next job if it doesn't work out as planned, which they might do anyway after a number of years. Thus, the entrepreneur is key. Or in the words of Annona fund manager Walter Hetterschijt, *'we invest as much in the entrepreneur as in the plan'*.

Why don't we write business plans anymore? There are millions of entrepreneurs, most of whom are convinced their business will work and can tell a convincing story. Unfortunately, very few have what it takes to establish a successful, medium-sized business. The challenge for any investor is to find out who does, and as efficiently as possible. Unfortunately, a business plan is one of the few means available for this selection procedure. The value of a good business plan is not only that it gives the business direction and can be used to secure funding, but that it forces the writer to do proper research and calculations to check his assumptions. It takes a good entrepreneur to write a good business plan. By writing a business plan for an entrepreneur, the investor denies himself this important selection mechanism. And what true entrepreneur wants to execute a plan developed by someone else? Finally, it is simply too expensive to write a good business plans for someone else. Good plans tend to be based on years of experience and experiments.

The challenge: "how do we find good entrepreneurs with a limited budget?"
The ongoing challenge we have faced since the start of Annona is how to find good entrepreneurs with good business plans in an efficient manner. In 2009, we estimated that as many as 400 investment opportunities might need to be evaluated in order to find 15 worthwhile investments. Two years later, we have found this to be true. Although a well-structured evaluation procedure and strict evaluation criteria and tools were developed too manage this 'investment funnel', managing the investment funnel has proven to be a balancing act between effectiveness and efficiency. If we do a quick and strict selection early on, little time is wasted on unfeasible plans, but we may end up with too few investments because good opportunities were wrongly rejected. The other approach – a more detailed evaluation early on – may mean too much of our budget is used on evaluating plans with too little potential.

Unfortunately, evaluating is not a matter of simply ticking boxes, because the perfect plan that meets all criteria doesn't exist. Each entrepreneur will need assistance and support to improve the plan to a level that will satisfy investors. To complicate matters, some people can be brilliant entrepreneurs but cannot write well, while a great-looking plan from a smooth talker may be based on ill-conceived assumptions. Background research is always needed to verify the plan and the skills of the entrepreneur. Evaluating proposals is therefore not only a matter of evaluating the business plan, but also the underlying 'intrinsic' business concept, the entrepreneur, and the amount of time it will cost to bring the business plan up to standard, including time spend on verifying the content. Sometimes, good-looking plans need to be rejected, because verification will be too time consuming.

We have also found that there is a tension between basing decisions on case-specific facts and heuristics. Heuristics is a method of quick decision-making with incomplete information, using intuitive judgment, common sense, educated guesses and "rules of thumb". Given the limited budget and the many business plans we receive, we are forced to rely heavily on heuristics. Though facts are better, heuristics are not necessarily a bad method of decision-making. They tend to be built on experience and knowledge obtained in similar cases, such as described in this book. Furthermore, some things are difficult to translate into objective facts. The ability of the entrepreneur is probably the most difficult; often you have the feeling they are or are not capable of building the business, despite what their CV and reputation tells you. Most successful businessmen will tell you that their 'gut feeling' is the most important criteria. On the other hand, instincts can be wrong. We have often shared the feeling with an entrepreneur that a business idea is great, until we did a simple competitive cost price calculation that proved us wrong. The challenge is to trust your instinct, but also force yourself to do fact-finding.

Because heuristics are necessary for efficient decision-making, it is important to make them more conscious, objective, complete, knowledge-based and consistent decision processes, by using your experiences. We have done a fair amount of reflection and documentation of our own experiences and those of other investors: Why did the business go bankrupt? Why was the plan rejected by the investors? Which criteria are used by others and why? We then tried to translate these experiences into selection criteria, tools and business plan templates. For example, we analysed the main reasons why we rejected over 100 business plans over the past years, and compared these with experiences of other investors. From there, we developed eligibility criteria against which each incoming investment opportunity is judged.

Common problems with business plans

We realized that many of the reasons why investment opportunities are rejected are related to the fact that KIT is located in the Netherlands and we operate within a network of 'traditional' development aid. For example, many Europeans dream of starting a business in an African country with which they have an emotional, social or economic bond. They may be experienced business people or development consultants with impressive CVs. And because they are in Europe they find us through their social network. Unfortunately, they tend to lack experience with the specific product they want to produce. They also lack an essential element for an entrepreneur: knowledge of, and a network in, the country in which they want to operate. In many cases as well, they don't plan to reside in the country full-time but plan to hire a local manager and fly in. Typically, their plan is built on a few site visits, Google and interviews with some 'experts'. It is full of assumptions and unsubstantiated statements, such as: "the world market for this product is huge". That may be the case, but have they spoken to potential customers who said they are willing to buy? Do they know who their competitors are? Can they deliver a better product at a lower price than China can? Another popular assumption is: "there are mountains of unused raw material that one can just gather". Unfortunately, there is often a reason why no-one is using that raw material.

Main reasons why investment opportunities were rejected:

1. No proper market analysis
2. No entrepreneur
3. Unrealistic sourcing strategy for raw material
4. No clear business strategy based on competitive advantage
5. Entrepreneur lacks relevant sector and/or country experience
6. Limited poverty alleviation potential
7. Lack of focus and commitment of the entrepreneur (investment of own money and 100% time)
8. Lack of proper financial analysis (cost price calculation)
9. Lack of commercial focus (Development project goes commercial…)
10. Lack of other funding sources/ investors
11. Investment size is too small or too big
12. Risk profile doesn't match

Another problem category concerns investment proposals that are based on traditional development projects. The starting point is often a group of poor people engaged in an economic activity. In an attempt to improve their income, they are supported through free training, organizational capacity building and the provision of machinery, buildings, and an expat manager. Unfortunately, a proper economic analysis into whether the goods produced can compete with imports and other local manufacturers is often lacking. And if there happens to be a competitive advantage, the question is still whether 'the business' can afford all these fancy machines, skilled managers and consultants. Giving people 'a fishing rod instead of fish' may sound like a great idea, but research and calculations should first to confirm that they should be 'fishing' at all. Furthermore, people working in these projects tend to lack basic business skills and an entrepreneurial mindset. Increasingly, as the project draws to a close, NGOs and development consultants try to find an investor to turn the project into a business, which is not easy because there is often no entrepreneur to be found. In our experience, it is easier to make a profitable business more socially-responsible, than to turn a social development project into a profitable business.

A local network in the South is crucial

Based on our experiences over the last two years, we realized the importance of a network that can 'feed good opportunities into the investment funnel' and help with the evaluation. The higher the quality that enters at the outset, the lower the amount of time wasted on 'bad' opportunities. We also realized that those entrepreneurs who managed to find us in Amsterdam might be good at finding development grants, but not necessarily in building a business. So we asked ourselves the question: 'where does a real entrepreneur start to look for funding?' The answer, of course, was a local bank. These banks often refuse to provide loans, either because they do not understand the business or because the entrepreneur lacks collateral and equity. We now try to work together with local banks and with financial institutions that provide working capital to entrepreneurs and share our investment criteria. We exchange investment opportunities, share the due diligence and co-invest. We also work with progressive NGOs in Africa and Latin America whose staff are skilled in business economics and are actively trying to link real local entrepreneurs to investors. This approach has led to a marked increase in the quality of the investment proposals received and a reduction of the evaluation cost. The ideas these NGOs put forward have already passed several selection rounds and much of the background research has been done. These organizations have also helped us with the support and coaching of entrepreneurs.

Public funding is needed

Finally, we have learned that despite the abundance of investment capital, public funding is still needed. The search and evaluation costs and the administrative costs for investments in agricultural SMEs in the developing world are simply too high to be earned back on the limited size of the investment. Clearly, there is a reason that banks and venture capital funds are not active in this sector. Particularly in the first two years, when experience and the network need to be built up, costs are high. Where the management fee for most conventional investment funds is around 1% to 2% over the committed capital, a fund like Annona would need around 3% to 4%. Commercial investors are not likely to pay this.

Public funding is also needed because many SMEs in the agricultural sector in developing countries need investments in public goods to make them profitable. For example in some cases small-scale farmers need to be organised, trained and certified. In others, decentralized collection stations need to be set up. These kind of investments are difficult to recuperate from the business activities. In such cases public money is crucial, for example in the form of an NGO organizing and training the farmers, because without it a private entrepreneur would not be able to start the business.

New investments
The new approach has led to a number of new investments:

Elephant Pepper in Mozambique is an expansion of the existing business in Zambia, set up many years ago by a talented Australian entrepreneur. The company supplies chilli peppers to the famous Tabasco brand and to spice companies using outgrowers and a core farm. Annona took 25% of the shares, which enabled the launch of the Mozambican operations.

There were important lessons to be learned. For example, how to value an existing firm in Africa, where much of the capital lies in the business concept and the network and know-how of the owner? We also learned that KIT, in the role of mediator, and Annona as a funder, can negotiate on the amount of social impact: we wanted more outgrowers for the money. Another lesson was that not only do we evaluate the business, the business also evaluates us as a mediator and Annona as a funder. Attractive businesses may have several options, and will choose the funder that offers the best conditions for them.

Agrisul in Mozambique is a starting business managed by two experienced farmer-entrepreneurs who aim to build 1500 hectare sugar cane farm surrounded by 4500 ha of outgrower farms producing sugar cane, soy and chili peppers. The business plan was solid, so the main challenge was to get a clear overview of the social impact of the business, in particular because a South African-managed sugar cane plantation does not immediately evoke images of a social business. Nevertheless, with electricity and railway transport coming to the area soon, market access and irrigation potential will improve tremendously, even for those local farmers not engaged in the outgrower program. KIT played the role of coach to ensure the social impact became visible and tangible. This case clearly showed the need for a fund like Annona: even with a secure land title, 30 years of combined farming experience on the part of the owners and a long-term contract with the sugar mill in place, local banks still required 27% interest and 150% collateral.

Agritrade in Bolivia is an existing specialty coffee business that buys from small-holder farmers. The company wanted to expand into peanuts, which originate from Bolivia. KIT has linked the business to Intersnack, a large Dutch importer that is willing to pay a price premium for the unique peanuts from this region, and was even willing to co-invest to make it happen. As of end-2010, the Bolivian peanuts will be in the market under a special brand. The challenge here was how to structure the business with its two separate activities, when Intersnack was only willing to invest in peanuts.

Virmax in Colombia is an existing business that buys specialty coffees from small-holder farmers in Colombia and Ecuador, and markets them in the US and Europe. The two young Colombian entrepreneurs, both with MBAs, managed to produce a convincing business plan for the expansion of their business.

The future
Over the coming years, KIT will continue to look for new investments for Annona and work with entrepreneurs to get their plans accepted by the investment committee. KIT will also continue to critically reflect on its own experiences and those of other funds. Questions that will be crucial are:

- Does our selection procedure lead to investments in economically-feasible companies?
- Do our investments have more social impact per invested euro than classic development projects?
- What is the return on investment compared to other investments, in different economic sectors, countries and investment vehicles?

Ultimately, we hope to be able to prove that profitable business and poverty alleviation go together.

Resources

Belt. J. and Spierenburg, M. (2010) 'Public-Private Partnerships in Rural Development, Downplaying the Role of Politics and Power Relations', in T.Dietz, A.Habib and H.Wells (eds) Governance and Development in Southern Africa. Proceedings from the third DPRN regional expert meeting on southern Africa, page 3-22, Rozenberg Publishers, Amsterdam.

Berdegué, J.A., Biénabe, E. & Peppelenbos, L. 2008, Keys to inclusion of small-scale producers in dynamic markets - Innovative practice in connecting small-scale producers with dynamic markets, International Institute for Environment and Development (IIED), London, UK.

Boomsma, M. 2008. Practices and challenges for businesses and support agencies. In Bulletin 385 - Sustainable procurement from developing countries. KIT Publishers.Boomsma, 2009

Boomsma, M. (2009) The Annona investment fund Poverty reduction through a private equity fund: a promising dream or an already existing reality? A business case for the University Cambridge Programme for Sustainability Leadership (PCSB).
http://www.oecd.org/dataoecd/43/63/36427804.pdf

Heslin, Peter A. and Ochoa, Jenna D., Understanding and Developing Strategic Corporate Social Responsibility. Organizational Dynamics, Vol. 37, pp. 125-144, 2008. Available at SSRN: http://ssrn.com/abstract=1149001

Humphrey, J. & H. Schmitz. 2000. Governance and Upgrading: Linking Industrial Cluster and Global Value Chain Research. In IDS Working Paper 120. Institute of Development Studies: University of Sussex and Institute for Development and Peace: University of Duisburg

Humphrey, J. & H. Schmitz. 2002. Developing Country Firms in the World Economy: Governance and Upgrading in Global Value Chains. 35. Duisburg: Institüt für Entwicklung und Frieden der Gerhard-Mercator-Universität Duisberg.

KIT, Faida MaLi and IIRR (2006) Chain Empowerment: Supporting African Farmers to Develop Markets. Royal Tropical Institute, Amsterdam; Faida Market Link, Arusha; and International Institute of Rural Reconstruction, Nairobi.
http://www.mamud.com/Docs/chains.pdf .

KIT and IIRR (2010) Value Chain Finance: beyond Microfinance for Rural entrepreneurs. KIT Publishers, Amsterdam.

Laven, A. (2010) The Risks of Inclusion. Shifts in governance processes and upgrading opportunities for small-scale cocoa farmers in Ghana. KIT Publishers. Thesis. AMIDSt, University of Amsterdam.

Peppelenbos, L. and Mundy, P. (eds) (2008) Trading Up: Building Cooperation between Farmers and Traders in Africa. Royal Tropical Institute, Amsterdam, and International Institute of Rural Reconstruction, Nairobi.
http://www.kit.nl/smartsite.shtml?id=SINGLEPUBLICATION&ItemID=2501.

E. S. Savas (2005) Privatization in the City: Successes, Failures, Lessons (Washington, DC: CQ Press, 2005), chapter 1

Ton, G., G. Hagelaar, A.Laven, and S.Vellema (2008) Chain Governance, Sector Policies and Economic Sustainability in Cocoa. Markets, Chains and Sustainable Development Strategy and Policy Paper 12, Wageniningen UR.

Tennyson, R. and L. Wilde (2000) *The Guiding Hand: Brokering partnerships for sustainable development*, New York, NY: United Nations Department of Public Information.

Wennink, B., Nederlof, S, and Heemskerk, W. (eds.) (2007) access of the poor to agricultural services. The role of farmer organizations in social inclusion. Bulletin 376. Development Policy & Practice. Royal Tropical Institute. KIT Publishers: Amsterdam.